Communications
in Computer and Information Science   309

Stefano Chessa   Stefan Knauth (Eds.)

Evaluating AAL Systems Through Competitive Benchmarking

Indoor Localization and Tracking

International Competition, EvAAL 2011
Competition in Valencia, Spain, July 25-29, 2011
and Final Workshop in Lecce, Italy, September 26, 2011
Revised Selected Papers

 Springer

Volume Editors

Stefano Chessa
Università di Pisa
Dipartimento di Informatica
Largo Pontecorvo 3
56127 Pisa, Italy
and
CNR, Istituto di Scienza
e Tecnologie dell'Informazione
via Moruzzi 1
56124 Pisa, Italy
E-mail: ste@di.unipi.it

Stefan Knauth
Hochschule für Technik Stuttgart
University of Applied Sciences
Schellingstr. 24
70174 Stuttgart, Germany
E-mail: stefan.knauth@hft-stuttgart.de

ISSN 1865-0929   e-ISSN 1865-0937
ISBN 978-3-642-33532-7   e-ISBN 978-3-642-33533-4
DOI 10.1007/978-3-642-33533-4
Springer Heidelberg Dordrecht London New York

Library of Congress Control Number: 2012947168

CR Subject Classification (1998): C.4, C.3, B.8.2, K.4.2, H.4.2, J.7, J.2, C.2.1, C.2.4, C.5.3

Typesetting: Camera-ready by author, data conversion by Scientific Publishing Services, Chennai, India

Printed on acid-free paper

Springer is part of Springer Science+Business Media (www.springer.com)

Preface

It is with great pleasure that we present this book, which summarizes the experience and results of the first EvAAL Competition. EvAAL aims at promoting a new approach to the evaluation and assessment of Ambient Assisted Living (AAL) systems and services, based on competitive benchmarking. In fact, the evaluation of AAL systems is a rather complex task, which will challenge researchers for years to come, due to their inherent complexity, but, on the other hand, this evaluation is paramount for the assessment of research results in this area. The approach promoted by EvAAL is to establish and refine over the years suitable benchmarks and evaluation metrics that are tried out on the field every year during the competition. The results of the competition are then discussed in a final workshop that is also the premise for the subsequent competition. In this respect, EvAAL represents an excellent opportunity to bring together different communities and research teams to work together on challenging and open problems, to evaluate various approaches, and to envision new research opportunities.

To deal with all such tasks while meeting the complexity of AAL systems, EvAAL proceeds gradually: the initial aim is to focus on the evaluation of AAL components, and only when methodologies, benchmarks, and criteria have become mature, will it move its focus towards services and complete systems.

In 2011, EvAAL focused on the problem of localization and tracking for AAL, as this is a key component for achieving context awareness. Recent years have witnessed an increasing trend of location-based services and applications. In most cases, however, location information is limited by the accessibility to Global Navigation Satellite Systems (GNSS), largely unavailable for indoor environments. To this end much research has been done in many research communities (in particular, sensor networks and ubiquitous computing communities) to provide techniques for localization and tracking in smart environments, and this EvAAL competion was aimed especially at those communities.

The competition was organized in two major events. The first event was the actual competition, which took place in Valencia, on July 25–29, 2011. During this event, the competitors were given 3 hours of time each to install, test, and uninstall their systems. The second event took place in Lecce on September 26th. This was the final workshop (hosted by the AAL Forum), where the competitors and organizers finally met and discussed the outcome of the EvAAL competition. The first EvAAL winners were also announced on this occasion.

The first two contributions in this book, written by members of the organization committees, describe the organization and technical aspects of the competition, while the other contributions, written by the competitors, provide a complete technical description of the competing artefacts and report on the experience lessons learned by the teams during the competition.

We wish to thank all organizers for their excellent work and for helping to make this EvAAL event a success, and the AALOA community (http://www.aaloa.org) and the universAAL project (http://www.universAAL.org) for the support they gave to this initiative.

However, a special word of thanks is due to all competitors, for the effort they made in the preparation of their systems for the competition and for the careful preparation of the papers describing their work, thus enabling a very interesting and lively competition and workshop.

July 2012   Stefano Chessa
                                                             Stefan Knauth

Organization

Organizing Committee

General Co-chairs

Stefano Chessa   University of Pisa and ISTI-CNR, Italy
Sergio Guillen   ITACA-UPV University of Valencia, Spain

Technical Program Committee Co-chairs

Rainer Mautz   ETH Zurich, Switzerland
Francesco Furfari   ISTI-CNR, Italy
Dario Salvi   Universidad politécnica de Madrid, Spain
Juan Pablo Lazaro   TSB Soluciones Tecnologicas, Spain

Local Committee

Juan Pablo Lazaro   TSB Soluciones Tecnologicas, Spain
Dario Salvi   Universidad politécnica de Madrid, Spain
Laura Belenguer   ITACA-UPV, Spain

Publication Chair

Reiner Wichert   Fraunhofer IGD, Germany

Publicity Chairs

Casper Dhal Marcussen   Region Syddanmark, Denmark
Francesco Potortì   ISTI-CNR, Italy

Program Committee

Bruno Andò   University of Catania, Italy
Paolo Barsocchi   ISTI-CNR, Italy
Philippe Canalda   University of Franche-Comté, France
Francesco Furfari   ISTI-CNR, Italy
Juan Pablo Lázaro   TSB Soluciones Tecnologicas, Spain
Ivan Martinovic   University of Kaiserslautern, Germany
Rainer Mautz   ETH Zurich, Switzerland
Filipe M.L. Meneses   University of Minho, Portugal
Adriano J.C. Moreira   University of Minho, Portugal
Francesco Potortì   ISTI-CNR, Italy
Dario Salvi   Universidad politécnica de Madrid, Spain
Saied Tezari   Fraunhofer IGD, Germany
Reiner Wichert   Fraunhofer IGD, Germany

Table of Contents

Comparing AAL Indoor Localization Systems 1
  *Paolo Barsocchi, Francesco Potortì, Francesco Furfari, and
  Alejandro M. Medrano Gil*

EvAAL, Evaluating AAL Systems through Competitive Benchmarking,
the Experience of the 1st Competition 14
  *Dario Salvi, Paolo Barsocchi, Maria Teresa Arredondo, and
  Juan Pablo Làzaro Ramos*

CapFloor – A Flexible Capacitive Indoor Localization System 26
  Andreas Braun, Henning Heggen, and Reiner Wichert

OwLPS: A Self-calibrated Fingerprint-Based Wi-Fi Positioning
System 36
  Matteo Cypriani, Philippe Canalda, and François Spies

The iLoc Ultrasound Indoor Localization System at the EvAAL 2011
Competition.. 52
  *Stefan Knauth, Lukas Kaufmann, Christian Jost, Rolf Kistler, and
  Alexander Klapproth*

Towards a Reusable Design of a Positioning System for AAL
Environments 65
  *Tomás Ruiz-López, Carlos Rodríguez-Domínguez,
  Manuel Noguera, and José Luis Garrido*

Precision Indoor Objects Positioning Based on Phase Measurements
of Microwave Signals 80
  Igor Shirokov

The n-Core Polaris Real-Time Locating System at the EvAAL
Competition.. 92
  *Dante I. Tapia, Óscar García, Ricardo S. Alonso, Fabio Guevara,
  Jorge Catalina, Raúl A. Bravo, and Juan M. Corchado*

Author Index... 107

Comparing AAL Indoor Localization Systems

Paolo Barsocchi[1,*], Francesco Potortì[1],
Francesco Furfari[1], and Alejandro M. Medrano Gil[2]

[1] ISTI Institute of CNR, Pisa Research Area, via Moruzzi 1, I-56124, Pisa, Italy
{paolo.barsocchi,potorti,furfari}@isti.cnr.it
[2] Life Supporting Technologies, Universidad Politècnica de Madrid, Avenida
Complutense n. 30, 28040, Madrid, Spain
amedrano@lst.tfo.upm.es

Abstract. Evaluating Ambient Assisted Living (AAL) systems is challenging due to the complexity and variety of solutions adopted and services offered. EvAAL is an international competition aimed to address this problem by evaluating and assessing the AAL systems components, services and platforms. In 2011 took place the first edition of EvAAL on the special theme of Indoor Localization and Tracking for AAL. This paper describes the technical aspects of the first edition of EvAAL and draws a roadmap for the future editions.

Keywords: AAL, localization, tracking.

1   Introduction

The evaluation and comparison of complex Ambient Assisted Living (AAL) systems is still far from being a reality [1]. On the other hand, the evaluation and assessment of components, services, and platforms for AAL systems is essential to ensure the progress, and, ultimately, the success of AAL technologies. EvAAL is an international competition on AAL supported by the AALOA association [2] and organized by the universAAL project [3]. It aims at advancing the state of the art in the evaluation and comparison of AAL platforms and architectures. EvAAL aims at contributing to AAL disciplines in the same way as other competitions have contributed to their respective areas. Under this respect EvAAL is inspired by successful competitions such as the Trading Agent Competition [4] (TAC) and DARPA Grand Challenge [5]. In contrast with the above mentioned competitions, and beyond supporting the growth of the AAL community, the main technical objectives of the competitions organized by EvAAL are to i) enable the comparison of different AAL solutions, ii) experiment with benchmarking and evaluation methods, iii) identify relevant AAL problems, requirements and issues, and iv) identify new and original solutions for AAL. EvAAL aims at enabling the comparison of different AAL solutions, by establishing suitable

---

* This work was supported in part by the European Commission in the framework of
the FP7 project universAAL under Contract 247950.

S. Chessa and S. Knauth (Eds.): EvAAL 2011, CCIS 309, pp. 1–13, 2012.

benchmarks and evaluation metrics that will be progressively refined and improved with time. In particular, EvAAL will focus not only on comparison of algorithms, but also of cost, deployment effort, user acceptance, and soon. EvAAL aims at generating an environment in which researchers, students, practitioners and industries can compare their solutions and build together methodologies and approaches that make such a comparison possible. Since at present the complexity of AAL systems makes not possible their full comparisons, EvAAL adopts a gradual approach, by dividing the problem into sub-problems, and by deferring the whole problem when the knowledge on AAL systems evaluation is more developed. Specifically, the first editions of EvAAL promote competitions on specific AAL components, in order to create data sets, benchmarks and evaluation methodologies. Then, based on the knowledge built in this phase, the subsequent EvAAL editions will focus on more complex (and possibly complete) AAL solutions. In the first edition it was chosen to organize a single track of competition on the topic "Indoor Localization and Tracking". Localization was chosen because it is a key component of many AAL services. Recent years have witnessed an increasing trend of location-based services and applications. In most cases, however, location information is limited by the accessibility to Global Navigation Satellite Systems (GNSS), largely unavailable for indoor environments. The scope of this competition is to award the best indoor localization system from the point of view of Ambient Assisted Living (AAL) applications. For organization reasons, EvAAL 2011 was split into two major events: the actual competition organized at the CIAmI Living Lab in Valencia (SP) [6], on the 27th-29th July, and the concluding workshop held in Lecce on the 26th of September (the workshop was a side event of the AAL Forum [7]). This gave the opportunity to each competitor to dispose of the living lab for a long time slot (3 hours), during which install, test and uninstall his/her system. This paper presents the technical aspects of this first EvAAL edition by discussing the evaluation criteria, the benchmarks and the results of the competition. In particular, Section 2 describes the benchmark tests we created to evaluate each competing localization system, section 3 shows the evaluation criteria used. Section 4 describes the localization system chosen as reference. The collected amount of data that are useful as benchmarks to the researcher communities are explained in section 5. While the protocol we followed during the competition is explained in section 6. The final results as well as the lesson learned in the first edition of EvAAL, and the conclusions are described at the end of this work.

2 Benchmarks

The score for measurable criteria (described later in section 3) for each competing artefact was evaluated by means of benchmark tests. For this purpose each competing team has been allocated a time slot of three hours, during which the benchmark tests had been carried out. The benchmark consists of a set of tests, each of which contributes to assessment of the scores for the artefact. For the evaluation, an Evaluation Committee (EC) was set up, composed of volunteer members of the Technical Program Committee. This EC was present during the competition and controlled all the operations to ensure a fair evaluation of each artefact. The time slot assigned to each competitor was divided in three parts:

- In the first part, the competing team deployed and configured their artefact in the living lab. This part should last no more than 60 minutes and its duration is measured in order to produce the score for installation complexity criteria (see section 3).
- In the second part, the benchmark is applied. During this phase the competitors had the opportunity to perform only short reconfigurations of their systems. In any case, this part should be concluded in 60 minutes.
- In the last part, the competitors must remove the artefact from the living lab in order to enable the installation of the next competing artefact.

Competing teams who failed to meet the deadlines in the first part have been given the minimum score for the installation complexity criteria. During the second part, the localization systems had been evaluated in two phases:

- Phase 1. In this phase each team had to locate the user (impersonated by an actor) inside an Area of Interest (AoI). The AoI in a typically AAL scenario could be inside a specific room (bathroom, bedroom), in front of a kitchen etc. Each system was requested to identify 5 Areas of Interest (AoI) (see Figure 1). The actor moved along predefined paths and stopped in each AoI for 30 seconds.

Fig. 1. The Areas of Interest deployed in the Living Lab

- Phase 2. In this phase the artefacts had to localize and track the actor that freely moved in the Living Lab. During this phase only the actor to be localized was inside the Living Lab. Each localization system produced localization data with a frequency of one new item of data every half a second. Each system was requested to track the actor along three different paths (Figure 2) which were the same for each test, and it was not disclosed to competitors before the application of the benchmarks. The first path was 36 steps length, the second path 52, and the last one 48. Moreover, all the paths were characterized by 3 waiting points, i.e. the actor stayed in the same position for 10 seconds. Each test lasted up to a couple of minutes.

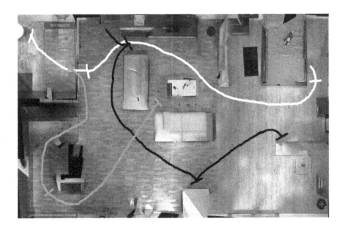

Fig. 2. The three different paths: path 1 (grey line), path 2 (white line), and path 3 (black line)

3   Evaluation Criteria

In order to evaluate the competing localization systems, EvAAL used a set of criteria weighted according to its relevance and importance for AAL applications. For each criterion, each competing artifact receives a score, that can be either measured by direct observation, or, when a direct measurement is not possible, it is determined by the evaluation committee. The criteria (along with the respective weights) are the following:

Accuracy (weight: 25%): each produced localization sample has been compared with the reference position and the error distance has been computed. Each localization system produced a stream of tuples, one sample every half a second. Specifically, the accuracy has been evaluated for each phase as:

- Phase 1: The accuracy in this case was measured as the fraction T of time in which the localization system provides the correct information about presence or not in a given AoI. The score for this phase was given by 10*T.
- Phase 2: The stream produced by competing systems has been compared against a logfile of the expected position of the actor. Specifically, we evaluated the individual error of each measure (the Euclidian distance between the measured and the expected points), and we estimated 75th percentile P

of the errors. In order to produce the score, P has been scaled in the range [0,10] according to the following formula:

$$AS = \begin{cases} 0 & \text{if } P > 4 \\ 10 & \text{if } P \leq 0.5 \\ 4*(0.5\text{-}P)+10 & \text{if } 0.5 < P \leq 2 \\ 2*(4\text{-}P) & \text{if } 2 < P \leq 4 \end{cases}$$

The score has been computed as the mean of the three scores obtained by each path.

The overall accuracy score has been computed as the mean of the two phases.

Installation Complexity (weight: 20%): a measure of the effort required to install the AAL localization system in a flat, measured by the EC as the total number of man-minutes of work needed to complete the installation. The time T was measured in minutes from the time in which the competitor enter in the living lab to the time when they declare they completed the installation (no further operations/configurations of the system will be admitted after that time), and it was multiplied by the number of people N working on the installation. The parameter T*N was translated in a score (ranging from 0 to 10) according with the following formula:

$$ICS = \begin{cases} 10 & \text{if } T*N \leq 10 \\ 10*(60\text{-}T^*N)\ /\ 50 & \text{if } 10 < T*N \leq 60 \\ 0 & \text{if } T*N > 60 \end{cases}$$

User Acceptance (weight: 20%): expresses how much the localization system is invasive in the user's daily life and in particular the impact perceived by the user. This criteria is qualitative and was evaluated by the EC taking into account a predefined list of questions.

Availability (weight: 15%): fraction of time the localization system was active and responsive. The availability A is measured as the ratio between the number of produced localization data and the number of expected data. In both, first and second phases, each localization system was expected to provide one sample every half a second, hence the number of expected samplings is given by the double of the test duration in seconds. The values of availability AvS has been translated into a score (ranging from 0 to 10) according to the following formula:

$$AvS = 10*A$$

Integrability into AAL Systems (weight: 10%): The score ranging from 0 to 10 was given by the EC according with the following list:

- 2 points for availability of libraries for integration;
- 2 points for use of open solutions for libraries;

- 2 points for use of standards;
- 2 points for availability of tools for testing/monitoring the system;
- 1 point for availability of sample applications;
- 1 point for availability of documentation.

4   Reference Localization System

The reference localization system is essential to measure the accuracy of the competing systems. In fact, the *accuracy* is defined as a statistic associated to the distance from the real position of the user and the estimated one, and the real position must be reliable and consistent. For this reason, the reference localization system was composed by predetermined coordinates of the paths followed by the actor during the competition. As shown in Figure 3, the Living Lab's floor was covered with red and blue marks (for the right and left foot, respectively) that show where the actor had to step on. The synchronization between the steps and the evaluation tool was guaranteed by a digital metronome that indicated the right cadence (one beep one step). In this way we guaranteed that the actor repeated the same paths at the same speed for every competitor.

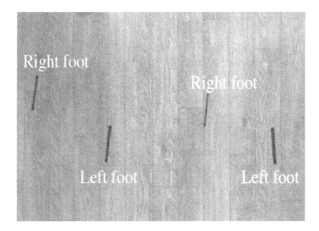

Fig. 3. The reference localization system: the blue marks are related to the left foot while the red ones are related to the right foot

5   Datasets Gathering

During the competition, we collected a large amount of data that are useful as benchmarks to researcher communities who can simulate and test their solutions. The benchmarks collected during EvAAL are particularly interesting as they were collected in a realistic environment with little or no prior preparation.

During the competition universAAL [3] has been used as the software platform to send and store localization events. Competitors were provided with a full running universAAL environment, in addition to a couple of competition specific modules that were developed. These packages include: the competition ontology, as universAAL is a semantic based framework, we had to specify the common semantics for all test runs; and a context provision module, which will make use of the specific semantics to provide location context events. Competitors had two alternatives to interface with the latter module, the primary option being a Java interface that could be imported from any Java project (see figure 4), the second being a simple TCP socket interface with a standard command line like protocol, which could be used by any implementation method used.

The use of universAAL enabled competitors to communicate with the local server, by means of simple localization context events, without any special configuration. UniversAAL will resolve problems like node discovering and inter node communication. In this first competition only basic features of universAAL were used. Based on experience, further competitions will employ broader use of universAAL features.

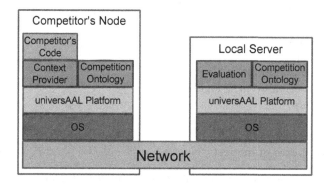

Fig. 4. Communication stack between competitor's node and the local server. Competitors are provided with all modules, even a template and sample of competitor's code.

Locally in the Living Lab a server program has been prepared as a receiver of the contextual information (module labeled Evaluation in figure 4). The local server was in charge of synchronizing the benchmarks and computing the availability and accuracy metrics in real time. The synchronization with the actor's position is also done by the local server namely by the control of the digital metronome. This synchronization is critical for computing of evaluation metrics since these are based on real time information like availability or jitter and correlate with the current position in the reference system. Also in real time the local server displayed a visual comparison of the position provided by the competitors and the real data. This display is used to detect problems in the communication.

Both on the competitors' computer and on the local server logs were produced in a human readable textual format. Although the competition data is also recorded by the local server, the software provided to competitors logged the sent data too, in case of unforeseeable communication problems. The information collected thereby can be resumed as follows:

Competitors' logs:

– Instant of time when the event has been sent to the platform
– Instant of time when the event has been estimated by the competitor
– Area of interest detected by the competitor
– Position (x axis) measured in meters
– Position (y axis) measured in meters

Server logs also include:

– Date and time of the benchmark
– Time difference between competitor's clock and server clock (measured manually at every benchmark)
– Competitor's name
– Benchmark name
– Jitter values
    • min jitter value
    • max jitter value
    • expected period of localization events
– Every localization event is logged with
    • timestamp
    • if it has been accepted or discarded by the jitter algorithm
    • expected coordinates (x,y)
    • expected area of interest

The complete data set has been also rearranged in a spread sheet that computes metrics and shows significant graphs about the actual and estimated position for every benchmark.

6   Methodology

The methodology followed to setting up the competition can be divided into three phases, namely preparation, execution and spreading knowledge.

Preparation. In this initial phase the benchmark and the evaluation criteria have been selected. This phase is probably the most delicate one, in fact, the choice of a benchmark/evaluation criteria with respect to another can lead to a different final result. Both, the benchmarks and the evaluation criteria, have been chosen according with the selected AAL scenario (Section 2 and 3). Moreover, the evaluation software that will be used during the competition is developed and tested. During this phase a call for competition has been spread, receiving 10 submissions where each competitor described its localization system. Through a peer-review process, 6 of the 10 proposed localization systems have been selected for the competition.

Execution. We defined a protocol that was followed for each competitor, and a member of the EC was responsible of making sure that all the steps are properly followed. The protocol consists of 17 steps:

1. When the competitor arrives the EC chair explains the protocol
2. The carpet of the Living Lab was covered before the competitor's arrival. This guarantee that all the competitors don't know the chosen paths before that the installation of their devices is completed.
3. All the members of the EC should be present observing that the rules of the competition are satisfied.
4. In order to produce the metadata for the datasets we measure the position of each device deployed in the Living Lab.
5. We measure the time necessary to deploy the localization system (installation time) in order to evaluate the ICS.
6. We unfold the carpet of the Living Lab
7. The integration between the competitor's software and the evaluation tool is performed
8. Only the actor will be inside the Living Lab during the evaluation phase, and the competitor as well as the EC will be outside.
9. All the evaluation phases, composed by the benchmarks defined in Section 2 will be recorded
10. The evaluation phase start and the evaluation tool will produce the scores relative to the accuracy and availability. These scores will be given follow the evaluation criteria described in Section 3. Moreover, during the evaluation phase, a real time graph has been produced that indicated the path followed by the actor and the position estimated by the localization systems (figure 6), and the estimated area of interest (figure 5).
11. The competitor will be interviewed regarding the integrability aspects (Section 3)
12. The EC will give the score about integrability (Section 3)
13. Each member of the EC give its own score about the user acceptance (Section 3)
14. The final score has been computed exploiting all the computed scores
15. The competitors answer to the questionnaire about the organization of the EvAAL competition
16. In order to collect the datasets the competitor gives to the organizer the intermediate data produced during the evaluation phase.
17. We fold the carpet of the Living Lab hiding, to the next competitors, the paths that the actor will perform during the evaluation phase

Spreading Knowledge. The last phase is related to the organization of a dedicated workshop where the proposed localization solutions are presented. The reason for separating the two phases (execution and spreading knowledge) was that, during the competition, the competitors where admitted one by one to

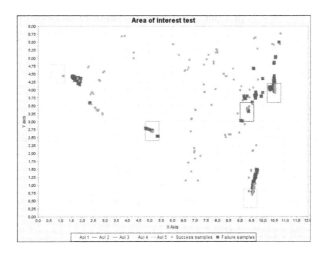

Fig. 5. Real-time graph of the actual and estimated Area of Interest

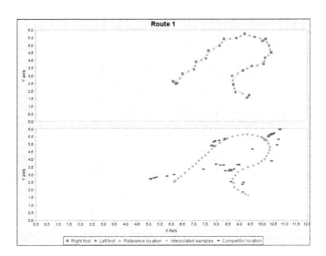

Fig. 6. Real-time graph of the actual (green points) and estimated coordinates (red points)

the living lab: each competitor was given a three hour time slot during which the system was installed and tested, and competitors did not have the opportunity to meet and discuss. The results obtained (datasets, description of the systems used by the competitors, benchmarks, Toolkit development, etc..) where presented later at the EvAAL workshop where competitors were also invited to describe their systems. The AAL Forum was chosen as hosting conference for the EvAAL Workshop because it is a major, annual conference of the Ambient Assisted Living Joint Programme, it has a large audience interested in AAL, and it gives a considerable attention to the most recent EU initiatives. For these reasons, it may provide to EvAAL the appropriate visibility in the scientific and industrial communities working on AAL.

7   Results

At the Ciami Living lab 6 teams challenged themselves at the competition, namely n-core Polaris (from the University of Salamanca) [8], AIT (from Austrian Institute of Technology) [9], iLoc (from Stuttgart University of Applied Sciences and iHomeLab at Lucerne University of Applied Sciences) [10], OwlPS (from University of Franche-Comte) [11], GEDES-UGR (from University of Granada) [12], and SNTUmicro (from Sevastopol National Technical University) [13]. Tables 1 and 2 summarize the scores of the different competitors. In particular, the n-Core system reached a best overall score, since it received the best score for availability, installation complexity and user acceptance. Since this localization system is based on Received Signal Strength (RSS) the accuracy score was third with respect to the other systems. The best localization system with respect to the accuracy score was AIT with the infrared technology, followed by the ultrasound devices of iLoc. The n-Core team won since it was the system that, on average, obtained a high score in all the metrics, while AIT and iLoc obtained low scores for availability and installation complexity, respectively.

Table 1. The measurable metrics: accuracy, availability and installation complexity

Competitor	Accuracy	Availability	Installation Complexity
n-Core [8]	5,96	9,88	10
AIT [9]	8,45	1,37	6,8
iLoc [10]	7,80	9,39	0
OwlPS [11]	1,37	9,43	8,5
GEDES-UGR [12]	1,81	9,02	0
SNTUmicro [13]	0	0	10

8   Lesson Learned

The first edition of EvAAL involved the participation of a good number of teams, and provided many feedbacks to the organizers for the next editions.

Table 2. The final scores and the jury decision scores (user acceptance and integrability)

Competitor	User Acceptance	Integrability in AAL	Final score
n-Core [8]	7.6	6.5	7.14
AIT [9]	6,88	8,5	5,90
iLoc [10]	5,88	4,5	4,98
OwlPS [11]	6,5	1	4,85
GEDES-UGR [12]	6	10	4,00
SNTUmicro [13]	4,38	3	3,17

The *Preparation* phase is the most delicate one, in fact the choice of the benchmarks and evaluation criteria for AAL applications is essential for the organization of the competition. These choices could be open not only to the organization committee but also to the competitors, that can give a quick feedback to the organizers on the substance of the proposal.

The *Execution* phase is the most important one, that will constitute the success or not of the competition. We highlighted that, in order to have success, the hosting structure (the living lab in our case) must guarantee the complete execution of the competition, and the integration between the competitor's software and the evaluation tools. To do that the structure must be able to resolve all the possible issues and to spare no effort in the overall organization.

The main trouble of the *Spreading knowledge* phase is the choice of an appropriate hosting conference able to offer logistics and publication facilities, a large audience interested in AAL, and a considerable attention to the most recent AAL initiatives.

9   Conclusions

Feedbacks from competitors and workshop audience were encouraging, for this reason we are currently planning EvAAL 2012, which will open to new tracks (while keeping indoor localization). In order to improve EvAAL we have prepared and distributed a call for ideas aimed at researcher, technician, or even user. The purpose of the call for ideas is to collect suggestions for the improvement of the technical and organization aspects of EvAAL, and to collect proposals for new topics. We conclude with our warm inviting everybody to help us make EvAAL a stable and widely recognized event for AAL. Further reading about the organization aspects of the competition are available on the official EvAAL website [14].

References

1. Connelly, K., Siek, K., Mulder, I., Neely, S., Stevenson, G., Kray, C.: Evaluating pervasive and ubiquitous systems. IEEE Pervasive Computing 7, 85–88 (2008)
2. AALOA association, http://www.aaloa.org

3. EU FP7 universAAL project, http://www.universAAL.org
4. Trading Agent Competition (2010), http://www.sics.se/tac/
5. DARPA Grand Challenge (2007),
   http://www.darpa.mil/grandchallenge/index.asp
6. CIAmI Living Lab., http://www.ciami.es/valencia/
7. AAL Forum, http://www.aalforum.eu
8. n-Core, http://n-core.info/
9. Fuxreiter, T., Mayer, C., Hanke, S., Gira, M., Sili, M., Kropf, J.: A modular platform for event recognition in smart homes. In: 2010 12th IEEE International Conference on e-Health Networking Applications and Services (Healthcom), pp. 1–6 (July 2010)
10. Knauth, S., Jost, C., Klapproth, A.: iLoc: a localisation system for visitor tracking and guidance. In: Proceedings of the Embedded World Conference, Nuremberg, Germany (March 2009)
11. Cypriani, M., Lassabe, F., Canalda, P., Spies, F.: Wi-Fi-based indoor positioning: Basic techniques, hybrid algorithms and open software platform. In: 2010 International Conference on Indoor Positioning and Indoor Navigation (IPIN), pp. 1–10 (September 2010)
12. Ruiz-Lòpez, T., Garrido, J.L., Rodrìguez-Domìnguez, C., Noguera, M.: Sherlock: A Hybrid, Adaptive Positioning Servicebased on Standard Technologies. In: AAL Forum Proceedings (September 2011) (to appear)
13. Shirokov, I.B., Ponyatenko, A., Kulish, O.: The measurement of angle-of-arrival of microwave in a task of precision landing of aircraft. In: Electromagnetics Research Symposium, July 26, Cambridge, USA, pp. 175–181 (2008)
14. EvAAL web site, http://evaal.aaloa.org/

EvAAL, Evaluating AAL Systems through Competitive Benchmarking, the Experience of the 1st Competition

Dario Salvi[1], Paolo Barsocchi[2],
Maria Teresa Arredondo[1], and Juan Pablo Làzaro Ramos[3,*]

[1] Life Supporting Technologies, Universidad Politècnica de Madrid
{dsalvi,mta}@lst.tfo.upm.es
[2] ISTI Institute of CNR, Pisa Research Area, via Moruzzi 1, I-56124, Pisa, Italy
j.lazaro@tsb.es
[3] Tecnologìas para la Salud y el Bienestar, Valencia
paolo.barsocchi@isti.cnr.it

Abstract. As Ambient Assisted Living (AAL) emerges as a need for our ageing societies, many barriers are still in place against its wide adoption. One of the main issues related to the creation of an AAL market is the lack of consensus around well established technologies which should effectively cover real needs of the population. EvAAL (Evaluating AAL Systems Through Competitive Benchmarking) is a newborn initiative aimed at evaluating solutions related to Ambient Assisted Living by organizing annual international competitions. Its main objectives are the creation of a community of stakeholders around AAL and the creation of metrics and benchmarks for both innovative prototypes and commercial solutions. EvAAL focuses not only on comparison of algorithms or specific hardware issues, but also of user acceptance, deployment and installation effort, integrability, etc. In its first versions, the competition is focusing on specific technical aspects of AAL but aims, in the near future, at joining heterogeneous "ambient" technologies in a common evaluation framework. In July 2011, the first EvAAL competition took place in Valencia, Spain, on Indoor Localization and Tracking for AAL. This paper describes how EvAAL is designed, its principles and how it is internally organized, and goes though an evaluation of this structure though the experience gained during the first competition.

Keywords: AAL, competition, indoor localization.

1 Introduction

Demographic changes are drastically affecting our societies. Our ageing population is having considerable consequences for public services, which have to be

---

* We would like to thank the whole universAAL Consortium for their valuable contribution for the realization of this work. This work was supported by the European Commission under the universAAL FP7-247950) within the 7th Research Framework Programme.

S. Chessa and S. Knauth (Eds.): EvAAL 2011, CCIS 309, pp. 14–25, 2012.
© Springer-Verlag Berlin Heidelberg 2012

deeply improved if their sustainability has to be reached. We need to motivate and assist elderly people to stay active longer in the labour market, live healthier, avoid social exclusion and keep them independent as long as possible. It is recognised that Information and Communication Technologies (ICT) offer a big opportunity for achieving these goals. The convergence of these technologies is often referred as Ambient Assisted Living (AAL) and is based on the following enabling technologies:

- sensing users and their environment,
- reasoning about users' situation,
- acting in reaction to the detection of a situation,
- communicating among different systems and applications,
- interacting with the user in a easy and effective way.

AAL is believed to be a major player in the future of our ageing society, such that the European Commission has been financing research and innovation in the Ambient Assisted Living Joint Programme[1] with 700 millions of Euro from 2008 to 2013.

AAL is an emerging, multi-disciplinary, convergent area, whose complete adoption still faces many barriers. In the Ambient Assisted Living Roadmap[1], authors particularly identify, as technical issues, the impairment between real needs and proposed solutions and the lack of standards and references for technological design. Moreover, under the economical view, the lack of proven business models and the high cost of ad-hoc solutions are also pointed out as major problems. An open and cooperative ecosystem, where developers, service providers, device manufacturers, and the housing industry can join, would push the implementation of innovative AAL systems.

One of the ways to overcome these limitations is by comparing existing solutions in real world scenarios and creating consensus among stakeholders on the adoption of the most efficient ones.

For this reason, as an initiative proposed by the universAAL FP7 project[2] and promoted by the AAL Open Association[3], a competition about AAL systems has been launched in 2011[2].

EvAAL[4] (Evaluating AAL Systems Through Competitive Benchmarking) is an international competition aimed at benchmarking both advanced prototypes and commercial products for the Ambient Assisted Living domain. Its main technical objectives are to:

- Enable the comparison of different Ambient Assisted Living (AAL) Solutions,
- Experiment with benchmarking and evaluation methods,
- Identify relevant AAL problems, requirements and issues,
- Identify new and original solutions for AAL.

---

[1] http://www.aal-europe.eu/

[2] http://www.universaal.org/

[3] http://www.aaloa.org/

[4] http://evaal.aaloa.org/

The first versions of EvAAL focuses on specific aspects of AAL, trying to identify a good set of tools and methodologies for assessing them. In a later stage, the aim will be joining these aspects, first two by two, and, eventually, in a unified AAL scenario. The aspects the competition will cover are the ones that define AAL itself, as mentioned before: *sensing* (e.g. effectively collecting heterogeneous context information), *reasoning* (e.g. transforming context data into knowledge), *acting* (e.g. environmental control through actuators), *communication* (e.g. sensor networks and distributed systems) and *user interaction* (e.g. ubiquitous and multi-modal user interfaces).

The first version of the competition, run in 2011, had Indoor Localization and Tracking as its theme. Localization is a key component for achieving context-awareness. In most cases, however, position information is limited by the accessibility to Global Navigation Satellite Systems (GNSS), largely unavailable for indoor environments. The scope of the competition was to award the best indoor localization system from the point of view of Ambient Assisted Living (AAL) applications. Both academic and industrial research communities were invited to participate and a benchmarking methodology had to be set-up to compare their solutions.

This paper describes the experience of this first competition, under the point of view of its design, organization, and financing. Technical details about evaluation metrics and tools are not covered in this work.

2   The EvAAL Competition

2.1   Identifying Best Practices

The design of the competition has been inspired by other initiatives in the computer science field. Some past and current competitions have been analyzed in order to identify successful practices, specifically: the Trading Agent Competition[3], the DARPA Grand Challenge[4], the International Collegiate Programming Contest[5], the International Olympiad in Informatics [6], the Google Code Jam[5] and the CONNECT Code-a-Thon Challenge[6].

The result of this analysis was the following set of requirements EvAAL should fulfil.

1. Regarding costs, the preferred solution is to involve a sponsor, in case this option failed, the organizing institutions should assume the costs at least of the set-up and some travel expense, and, as the last option, a fee can be asked to participants.
2. The competition should have a clear and structured organization with different committees in charge of all the aspects of the competition (choosing the place, setting-up the call, defining the metrics, organizing the logistics, etc.).

---

[5] http://code.google.com/codejam
[6] http://hit.fiu.edu/challenge.htm

3. Participant teams should provide basic information of the competing artefacts in the form of a paper, so that submissions could be selected if they
   are too numerous to be hosted.
4. Competitors should integrate their software with a common benchmarking
   system.
5. A panel of evaluators should assess aspects that are not directly measurable
   with benchmarks.
6. The results of the competition should be made public in a hosting conference,
   the competition itself could be run together with the conference.
7. All the results and achievements of the competition should be publicly given
   to the research community and constitute a base for future developments of
   the competition.

2.2   The Target Groups

Different kind of stakeholders can be involved in the EvAAL competition. The
final objective of the competition is to promote valuable solutions that would be
adopted in the potential AAL market and join stakeholders around the adoption
of these solutions. In order to achieve this goal all the players of AAL should be
included.

Particularly the following figures can be interested in EvAAL: a) developers of AAL solutions and technologies in form of both hardware and software,
b) deployers of AAL solutions responsible for installation, configuration, cus-
tomization, and orchestration of integrated AAL applications, c) non-technical
end-users such as assisted persons and their caregivers, d) providers of external
services to the end-users that may acquire solutions provided by the developers
and use services provided by the deployers in order to set up an infrastructure
necessary for their business, e) supporting organizations and authorities that
deal with socio-economical and legal context of AAL.

Involving all these figures is extremely challenging. For this reason, the first
versions of EvAAL will mainly include technical players (developers and deployers) in order to firstly gain consensus on the adoption of common technologies,
and in a later stage, more complex scenarios which involve other players will be
set-up.

2.3   Internal Structure

EvAAL is managed by a *Steering Board* (SB), which is in charge of organizing
the competition annually. The SB is composed of 5 to 7 members from both
academia and industry, membership is free of charge and volunteer. Each year a
SB chair is elected to control the progress of the board. The chair decides the
agenda of the meetings and controls voting when decisions must be made.

The SB issues a call for ideas, which is addressed to all relevant stakeholders
in order to collect ideas about methods, issues to be studied and benchmarks
for the next competition. The call is disseminated in relevant channels such as
conferences and discussion fora, and a number of Special Themes are selected

among submissions. The selection is based on the quality of the submission, on the feasibility of the organization plan, on the availability of resources and on the scientific reputation of the proposers.

In this process, the SB is supported by an *Advisory Board*, which gives advice regarding the strategic decision-making process but does not have any authority to vote or to make decisions.

For each accepted Special Theme, the Steering Board then establishes one *Special Theme Chair* (STC) and one *Scientific Committee*, to lead the formation and running of the technical program. STCs identify candidates for the Scientific Committee, lead the preparation of the Call for Special Themed Competition, define the criteria for competitors selection and organize the selection of the competitors. STCs are also in charge of the competition session, including defining the spaces and logistics requirements, implementing the benchmarks and suitable tools and reporting the activities of the competition to the SB.

At the same time, the Steering Board nominates the *General Chair* and the *Organizing Committee* of the competition. The General Chair has the role of coordinating the Scientific Committees and the Organization Committee to ensure the success of the competition, while the Organizing Committee is responsible for the logistics issues of the whole competition. He or she has the ultimate responsibility for the success or the lack of thereof of any given competition in terms of 1) technical quality of the competition, 2) quality of the organization, 3) number of attendees and 4) satisfaction of the participants.

In order to ensure financial stability year after year, the SB elects a *Registration and Finance Chair* who manages the budget of the competition, collects fees, sponsorships and pays travel grants.

Within each local organizing committee a *Publicity Chair* a *Local Chair* and a *Publication Chair* are also nominated yearly. The Publicity Chair coordinates the advertisement of the competition and the dissemination of the call for competition. The Local Chair organizes the logistics of local competition, guarantees that all the needed equipments are provided locally, distributes information about the travel, the directions, visas etc and organizes the social events. If the competition results are presented in a hosting conference, the Publication Chair identifies a suitable conference and proposes it to the SB for acceptance. Then he/she manages the relationships with the conference, including the editing of papers describing the competing artifacts and their preparation in accordance to the format required by the conference proceedings.

The organization of EvAAL is sketched in figure 1.

2.4   Financing

EvAAL aims at collecting finances each year for running the competition from different sources. The main identified source is a sponsorship of some company or public entity which is interested in the topics of the competition. If the sponsorship is not found, or does not reach a sufficient amount of money to pay all the expenses, it is foreseen that the organizing institutions of the competition partially assume some costs like setting up the evaluation sites and personnel.

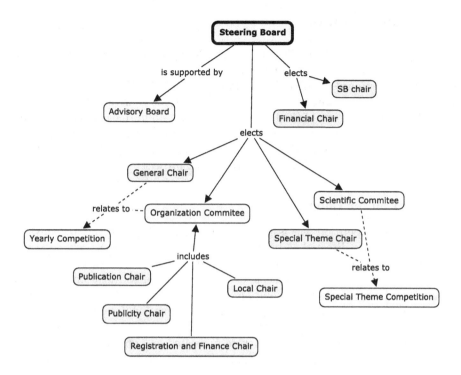

Fig. 1. Diagram of the internal organization of EvAAL

As a last resource competitors will be asked for a registration fee (situation that should be avoided to make the competitions more appealing).

The financing of the competition is pursued according to a specific budget plan that must be defined every year by the Registration and Finance Chair along with the General Chair and approved by the Steering Board. Typical costs to run a competition include:

- Logistics Costs, like catering service for the meals, social event, Living Lab infrastructures and personnel costs, reimbursement for the evaluation committee, conference material (city map, note block, etc.)
- Costs for benchmarks preparation, like developing the evaluation toolkit that allows applicants to integrate their systems, infrastructure setup (installation of servers, networks etc.), configuring and tuning the infrastructure
- Prize, to be given to the winner(s) of the competition
- Costs related to the publication of the results of the competition, like creating or updating a website, conference proceedings, special issues, etc.
- Publicity and dissemination costs, like sending invitations, producing brochures and leaflets, announcing the competition in conferences, etc.
- Competitors costs, like costs for adapting the solution to the EvAAL requirements, registration fees, travel costs, accommodation, meals, etc.

3   The 2011 Edition

The first version of EvAAL was run in July 2011 with a single Special Theme about indoor localization and tracking.

The Steering Board appointed Stefano Chessa (ISTI-CNR, Italy) and Sergio Guillèn (ITACA-UPV University of Valencia, Spain) as General and co-Chair of the EvAAL 2011, and established the Organization Committee and the Scientific Committee. The Scientific Committee was composed by experts in the field of localization and tracking coming from six different countries. Seven of the total 13 members where coming from the universAAL project.

3.1   The Call for Competition

The Call for Competition was issued by the Steering Board in the first days of April. The call was directed to individuals or groups working as a single team, from research institutes, academies and industrial companies. Candidate competitors were invited to submit a paper describing their localization system in terms of hardware, deployment, and algorithms and protocols used. Ten applications were received within the following month, from 7 different countries and underwent a peer review by the Scientific Committee members. Nine papers were accepted, three major revisions were requested and only one was rejected. Eventually, two competitors couldn't participate due to hardware problem and for commercial and internal issues, and one competitor was finally admitted as guest but not officially competing. The other six competitors were invited to participate in the competition itself. Table 1 shows the name of the competing teams and their nationalities.

Table 1. Accepted competing teams in EvAAL 2011

Team Name	Nationality
n-Core Polaris	Spain
iLoc	Germany, Switzerland
SNTUmicro	Ukraine
GEDES-UGR	Spain
AIT	Austria AIT
OwIPS	France

3.2   The Location: The CIAMI Living Lab in Valencia

The competition took place at the CIAMI Living Lab[7], in Valencia, Spain on the 27th-29th July, 2011. The Living Lab is an approximately 90 m^2 infrastructure that simulates the real environment of a citizen's home (a map of the lab is shown in Figure 2).

---

[7] http://www.ciami.es/valencia/

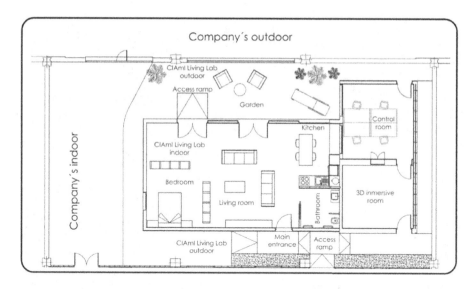

Fig. 2. The map of the CIAMI Living Lab

The place was chosen because it fulfilled the following requirements: it simulates a real house with separate environments (rooms); it has removable ceiling and floor; it provides networking facilities as ethernet and Wi-Fi; the surrounding environment is clean of radio frequency interferences; it has a continuous video recording system; a supporting team of people was available for installation and maintenance; side meeting rooms were available; it was possible to hide marks on the floor thanks to a removable carpet.

When preparing the competition, the Scientific Committee identified the need of having a reference localization system to compare competitors' data with. The system should have been able to precisely locate a human actor in movement. The requirements posed by the committee were a precision under 0.5 meters, little or no electromagnetic interferences, easy to install and deploy, easy to integrate with software systems. After an extensive research, it was decided to abandon the idea of an automatic localization system, and a more "manual" and transparent approach was taken.

During the benchmarks, a human actor walked a series of paths at a fixed speed, in the same amount of time, for any competitor. Each step of the path was marked on the floor and its coordinates were recorded on a sheet (figure 3 shows an example of a path). Competitors did not know the paths in advance, and could not see the paths during the installation of their systems (paths are covered with a plastic surface). A computer program, which the competitors were connected with, guided the human actor thanks to metronome-like sounds, and the estimated positions sent by the competitor, versus the one known a-priori, were compared.

Fig. 3. A reference path on the floor of the CIAMI Living Lab

The advantages of this approach were its transparency (no hidden or unknown technology was used), and the fact that it can be used in almost all environments without the need of any specific technology.

The software solution was based on the AAL programming platform developed in the universAAL project. Competitors were invited to integrate their systems with the universAAL middleware and publish localization events on the distributed environment it offered. The integration was simplified by providing an example application that hid the complexity of the universAAL platform, and the source code of the integration packet was made publicly available on a SVN repository[8].

3.3   The Publication of the Results

The EvAAL competition 2011 was not a public event, in fact competitors installed their systems separately and the evaluation of each system was done independently. The obtained results in terms of datasets, description of the systems used by the competitors, benchmarks, toolkit development, etc. were however made public.

---

[8] http://forge.universaal.org/gf/project/evaal/

All the results have been published in a dedicated workshop where competitors were invited to present their systems. The workshop was organized as a side event of the AAL Forum[9], which took place in Lecce, Italy, on the 26th of September 2011. The AAL forum is an annual conference of the Ambient Assisted Living Joint Programme (AALJP). The objective of the AAL Forum is twofold: on the one hand the conference aims to show the significant progresses made by the AALJP projects and its practical implications on the daily life of seniors. On the other hand a considerable attention is dedicated to the most recent EU initiatives, like the pilot European Innovation Partnership on Active and Healthy Ageing. The AAL Forum provided logistic facilities, publicity and dissemination and publication of the workshop proceedings.

3.4 Financing

The first edition of EvAAL run without any official sponsor.

Most of the logistics costs were covered by the CIAMI Living Lab, while some partners of the universAAL project contributed with force work, part of logistics and benchmarks preparation costs (including gadgets given to the competitors and the prizes), and the costs for the EvAAL workshop.

The prize of the competition consisted in a series of plates (for the first, second and third winners) officially given during the side event of the AAL Forum. The cost of prizes was covered by some partners of the universAAL project, which additionally, partially covered the competitor's costs by reimbursing their expenses for participating in the AAL forum up to a maximum of 800€. Competitors had to sustain their own expenses for participating in the competition in Valencia.

4 Evaluating EvAAL and Lessons Learnt

The measure of success of EvAAL depends on its ability of reaching its main objectives. In particular there are two kinds of objectives: one is the ability of EvAAL of supporting the growth of the community and to become widely recognized in the international community. The second is the ability of EvAAL to identify relevant AAL problems, requirements, and issues, and to propose new, original solutions and their evaluation.

Regarding the first point, there are some aspects that are not easily measurable in the short period, among these are the ability of EvAAL to foster the development of new research themes and related conferences, as well as the creation of a synergy among different stakeholders. On the other hand some aspects are objectively measurable, like the number of submissions to the Call for Ideas, the funding raised with sponsors, or the number of industries and service providers involved in the identification of special themes for the competition.

About the second aspect (the capability of identifying new issues and to evaluate solutions) there are no simple direct metrics. The growth of the community

---

[9] http://www.aalforum.eu/

around EvAAL gives an indirect indication of its technical quality, because if EvAAL fails to meet its technical objectives it will hardly be capable of gluing and keeping a large community.

Although it is not easy to evaluate the success of the first version of EvAAL without any other reference, facts indicate a fair success.

The event attracted a good number of teams from many EU countries with different solutions. This has been challenging for the EvAAL organizers in terms of providing fair benchmarking that allowed each competitor equal opportunities. The resulting approach favored real-world applicability, encouraging the competitors to adjust their systems in this regard. At the end of the competition an estimation of the costs was performed and the conclusion was that, without any further financing, the number of actual participants was a good compromise between costs and variety of competitors.

Moreover, EvAAL was assessed directly by their participants. At the end of the benchmarks, before un-installing all the appliances, a questionnaire was given to each team representative were to express their opinions about the event. The questionnaire was composed by both free text and structured questions, and comprised a section about the profiling of the competitor (industrial or research, skills, knowledge about AAL, etc.), a section about evaluating the organization of EvAAL and the fairness and technical quality of the benchmarks, and finally an evaluation of the integration software. The results of this questionnaire were more than satisfactory and the answer can be summarized as follows:

- All the competitors share the idea and the objectives of the EvAAL competition and are interest in the AAL applications and services.
- All the competitors are willing to participate in the next edition as competitors or as part of the scientific committee. For the next competition they propose some improvements of metrics and about the organization of the event (better schedule and exploration to the lab before the evaluation).
- The chosen Living Lab and the hosting facilities have been considered properly equipped and adequate for the EvAAL competition.

After the conclusion of the event all the processes were analyzed by the Steering Board and a set of recommendations were set-up for the future competitions. Particularly the following issues have been identified:

1. sponsorship should be found to finance at least the cost for participating in the competition in order to attract also competitors from far countries,
2. hiding the reference paths for every competitor is a hassle (it means covering and uncovering the entire floor per every competitor) and should be avoided. A possible improvement could consist in using wooden sticks that mark partial, straight paths, that could be placed and removed easily,
3. the integration software had some bugs and could not work properly for all the competitors. In the end system logs were used to retrieve data, but for the next versions a backup solution must be foreseen,
4. qualitative metrics should improve in order to be more reliable and should better support that both prototypes and commercial solutions.

5   Future Competitions

As AAL evolves with time, EvAAL shall evolve with it. For this reason the evaluation criteria and success metrics of EvAAL need to be periodically revised and updated. This role is assigned to the EvAAL Steering Board, which, to this purpose, also prepares, distributes and analyses evaluation forms to be distributed to the EvAAL attendees.

For the 2012 edition, a Call for Ideas was issued in September 2011, and closed in January 2012. Two Special Themes were chosen: one is an extension of the indoor localization track, which adds contextual information coming from the domotic appliances of the hosting Living Lab (the Smart House in Madrid, Spain). The second track is about activity recognition and will be hosted by the CIAMI Living Lab. The Special Theme Chairs and Scientific Committees of the tracks were also chosen accordingly.

At the time of writing the call for competition has already been issued[10] and submissions are being received.

References

1. van den Broek, G., Cavallo, F., Wehrmann, C. (eds.): AALIANCE Ambient Assisted Living Roadmap. Ambient Intelligence and Smart Environments, vol. 6. IOS Press (2010)
2. AAL Open Association: The AALOA manifesto
3. Wellman, M., Wurman, P., O'Malley, K., Bangera, R., de Lin, S., Reeves, D., Walsh, W.: Designing the market game for a trading agent competition. IEEE Internet Computing 5, 43–51 (2001)
4. Seetharaman, G., Lakhotia, A., Blasch, E.: Unmanned vehicles come of age: The DARPA grand challenge. Computer 39, 26–29 (2006)
5. Shilov, N.V., Yi, K.: Engaging students with theory through acm collegiate programming contest. Commun. ACM 45(9), 98–101 (2002)
6. Dagiene, V., Skupiene, J.: Learning by competitions: olympiads in informatics as a tool for training high-grade skills in programming. In: 2nd International Conference on Information Technology: Research and Education, ITRE 2004, June 28-July 1, pp. 79–83 (2004)

---

[10] `http://evaal.aaloa.org/current-competition/call-for-competition2012`

CapFloor – A Flexible Capacitive Indoor Localization System

Andreas Braun, Henning Heggen, and Reiner Wichert

Fraunhofer Institute for Computer Graphics Research - IGD
Fraunhoferstr. 5,
64283 Darmstadt, Germany
`{andreas.braun,henning.heggen,`
`reiner.wichert}@igd.fraunhofer.de`

Abstract. Indoor localization is an important part of integrated AAL solutions providing continuous services to elderly persons. They are able to fulfill multiple purposes, ranging from energy saving or location based reminders to burglary detection. Particularly useful are combined systems that include localization, as well as additional services e.g. fall detection. Capacitive sensing systems that allow detecting the presence of a body over distance are a possible solution for indoor localization that has been used in the past. However usually the installation requirements are high and consequently they are expensive to integrate. We propose a flexible, integrated solution based on affordable, open-source hardware that allows indoor localization and fall detection specifically designed for challenges in the context of AAL. The system is composed of sensing mats that can be placed under various types of floor covering that wirelessly transmit data to a central platform providing localization and fall detection services to connected AAL platforms. The system was evaluated noncompetitive in the 2011 EvAAL indoor localization competition.

Keywords: Indoor localization, capacitive sensors, fall detection.

1 Introduction

Indoor localization systems have a number of applications in AAL that are not directly visible to the user but are available to other services, e.g. lighting based on location or context-aware systems that may prevent burglary, e.g. if the system detects a person entering a space in the proximity of a window. It is preferable that those systems are unobtrusively integrated into the living space and provide a good recognition under many circumstances, e.g. looking at vision-based system the user may feel watched and systems may struggle on low light levels. We are proposing a system on floor level based on capacitive sensors that allow localization using low-intensity electric fields that detect the presence of a human body. They are invisible to the end-user and can be unobtrusively integrated into non-conductive materials. The focus of this system is flexibility using individual passive mats with electronic materials placed on the borders, allowing for easy maintenance and affordable

S. Chessa and S. Knauth (Eds.): EvAAL 2011, CCIS 309, pp. 26–35, 2012.

construction. Using a specific electrode configuration it is possible to customize each mat to room conditions by cutting off parts. Another advantage of this sensing system is that it can be used for other application scenarios, e.g. detecting the presence of a person lying on the floor to register falls.

2   Related Work

Capacitive sensors are a fairly old technology [1] able to detect the presence of an object by using the effect said object has on a generated electric field. It is most commonly used in finger-controlled touchscreen devices [2] and material detection in industrial applications [3].

Floors equipped with sensors that allow the detection of objects is an area that has been researched in the future. We can distinguish pressure sensing systems that detect weight distribution changes or presence sensing systems like the one proposed. One example for pressure sensing systems is the ORL active floor [4] that is based on tiles directly placed on pressure sensors and uses a Hidden Markov Model based approach to detect footsteps.

SensFloor [5] is a capacitive sensor based system comprised of carpet tiles with integrated electronics that wirelessly communicate with a central system. It is a precise system able to distinguish individual footsteps and has been marketed as fall detection system. Different to CapFloor it relies on a tile based system with active electronic components integrated into the carpet. While this approach provides a high precision the technology is complex and difficult to maintain in case of failing systems. CapFloor relies on electronics that are attached to the side of a floor and passive elements under different materials that is resistant to defects and can be modified easily.

3   CapFloor Hardware

The CapFloor prototype is based on the open source hardware CapToolKit[1] providing a control unit that supports up to eight sensor elements for capacitive sensing. The device is using a firmware that has been optimized for controlling the CapFloor. Additionally the system is available in several variants. One is transferring data via USB, the other uses an Arduino[2] system with attached XBee Shield[3] and Bluetooth Bee[4] to transmit the data using the Blutooth Serial Port Protocol. This second version is shown in Fig. 1.

---

[1] http://www.capsense.org

[2] http://www.adruino.cc

[3] http://www.arduino.cc/en/Main/ArduinoXbeeShield

[4] http://seeedstudio.com/wiki/index.php?title=Bluetooth_Bee

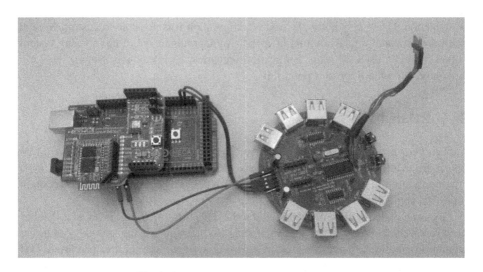

Fig. 1. CapToolKit with Bluetooth Arduino

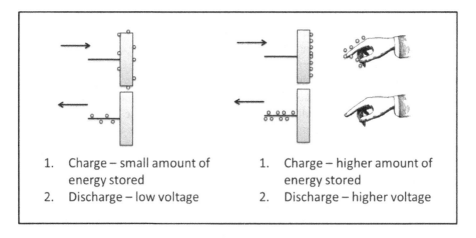

Fig. 2. Capacitive proximity sensor

The system is an 8-channel single-electrode capacitive proximity sensor controller. The working principle is shown in Fig. 2. Conductive, grounded objects that enter the electric field excited by the electrode are increasing the capacity of the electric field. The energy is highest if the object is large and the distance to the electrode is small. One very simple model is a two-plate capacitor, the capacitance C of which is given by the following equation with ε_o being the electrical constant, ε_r the relative permittivity between the plates, A the size of the plates and d the distance.

$$C = \varepsilon_0 \varepsilon_r \frac{A}{d}$$

Concerning the human body there is no analytical solution regarding the capacitance relative to an electrode [6]. Typically it is modeled using the two-plate model or considering the human body as a sphere.

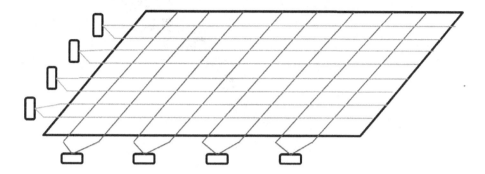

Fig. 3. Conceptual drawing of the CapFloor electrode & sensor configuration

For the prototype we are using passive floor mats of a rectangular shape equipped with active sensor elements on two adjacent outer sides. The size of the floor mats is variable and one mat is able to cover several square meters of floor, e.g. the prototype covers an area of approximately 6m².

The electrodes are applied in two layers that are insulated to each other by means of using insulated wire. Two wires are connected to each electrode in order to increase the spatial range of a single sensor. The achievable resolution is depending on the number of sensors that are placed on the side of a mat. Systems are available that provide measurements in the sub-millimeter range. Our application is considered to be tailored for a typical indoor localization task where we consider a resolution of approximately 50cm sufficient. This allows us to cover the 6m² area mentioned above with just eight sensors. The number of sensors and accordingly the distance between the wires has to be chosen in a way so the typical human foot will always be placed on a wire. While the technology allows detection along a certain distance this solution is preferable since the selected geometry for wiring has a considerable signal-to-noise ratio.

However this electrode configuration gives the possibility to adjust the shape of the floor mats without adaptation of the electronic configuration. The mats can be simply resized to almost any convex shape, e.g. to place them in the corner of a room or to fit several mats into one room. The cutting of the wires affects the sensor response, yet we can use compensation on the software side to account for the different response curves.

For easier installation the floor mats are designed to transmit the sensor data wirelessly to a central station, which is running the CapFloor Software. This minimizes the necessary wiring and thus avoids additional work and cost during the installation and guarantees an unobtrusive integration into the living space. For this wireless transmission we use the previously mentioned Bluetooth-based system on an Arduino microcontroller.

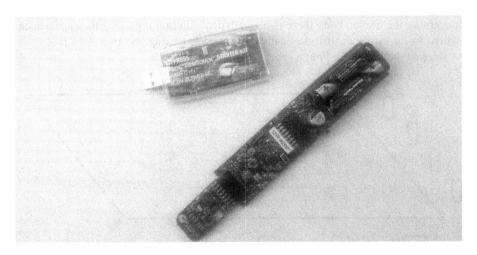

Fig. 4. Cypress wireless capacitive sensor CY3241

A further addition to our hardware platform is the support for small areas that are connected to a single capacitive sensor, in our case a Cypress wireless capacitive sensor as shown in Fig. 4. This allows us to equip small mats with a single wire electrode to provide localization on smaller areas that can be placed further away from the more sophisticated mats in regions where it is only required to know if it is currently occupied or not. Within those smaller mats no internal localization is possible.

4   CapFloor Software

The CapFloor Software is performing various tasks. Low-level data processing is used to improve the noisy sensor signals. It allows modeling the room from individual mats, taking into account shape and orientation. Signals from the different sensors are uniquely identified and used to create an overall picture for all equipped and modeled rooms.

The low-level data processing is consisting of the following parts:

- Average filtering of the sensor signals using a configurable amount of samples.
- Baseline calibration to determine the normal operating level of each sensor.
- Normalization based on the baseline and tracking of minimum and maximum measurements at run-time.

The software provides two main services. The localization service is providing other services with the position of a user in the current environment. This info is generated in a two-step process. The software individually performs individual localization for each mat. We use a weighted-average algorithm to determine the interpolated location in each sensor layer.

$$\bar{x} = \frac{\sum_{i=1}^{n} v_i x_i}{\sum_{i=1}^{n} v_i} \quad , \quad \bar{y} = \frac{\sum_{i=1}^{n} v_i y_i}{\sum_{i=1}^{n} v_i}$$

The resulting location $(\bar{x}, \bar{y})$ is calculated using the sums over sensor positions (x_i, y_i) and sensor values v_i as weight. This allows us to improve the resolution of the system that uses simple activity thresholds on the sensors.

If an object is detected the location is then mapped to the environment using knowledge of the mats position and orientation, as well as known parameters of the equipped space. This allows a global localization of objects and tracking their movement throughout the environment and over different mats.

Furthermore the system uses a rule-based heuristic system to improve the localization by ignoring impossible sensor readings (false-positives) and resolving ambiguous sensor readings. This component is using historical sensor and location data to evaluate the rule set. One example for false positive would be the registration of a person in the middle of a room without registering his entrance. In this case the system would discard the detected position unless the change is consistent over a certain amount of time. An example for ambiguous sensor data is distinguishing between several persons standing close to another and a single person lying which might cause similar sensor output. We resolve such situations by tracking the persons throughout the room - if there are three persons in one room and they are moving towards each other to a stand this will not be counted as a lying person. These rules are hardcoded into the system right now.

The second main service is fall detection. The signal generated by a lying person is significantly different from a walking person. This effect is using the combined measurements over several adjacent mats, to allow detecting falls that result in a person lying on several mats. This service can be connected to alarming services that ask the user if everything is well, or automatically call for help if a person is lying for a certain amount of time.

A challenging aspect of working with capacitive sensors is proper calibration. The signals vary based on the environment and also drift over time, e.g. caused by temperature or humidity changes. Both effects are taken into account in the created software, providing drift compensation over time, as well as a remote calibration. As shown in Fig. 5 the drift compensation is using two different patterns. The low baseline reset is started as soon as the sensor values drop below the baseline. A short-term sampling is following (to prevent outliers) and the baseline is set to the new smallest value. The threshold based sampling is adapting long-term changes of the baseline by using an activity threshold - a minimal value that is considered when a body is approaching the sensor - and a long-term sampling of sensor values that are below this threshold. The baseline is increased in that case.

The remote calibration is required when permanent changes are occurring in the environment, e.g. when new furniture is placed in the room. Affected individual mats or the whole room can be recalibrated to the new parameters by taking a larger number of samples and calculating a new baseline.

The capacitive sensor system has been connected as a service to the universAAL[5] AAL platform already in previous work implementing capacitive sensors into an occupation-detecting couch.

---

[5] http://www.universaal.org

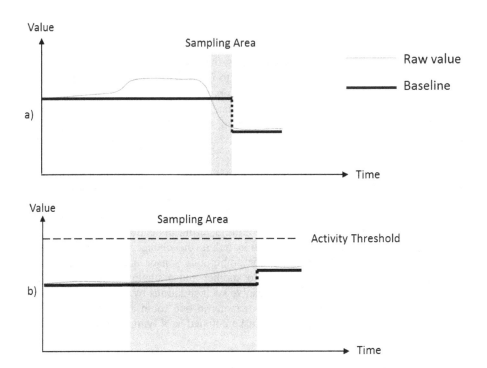

Fig. 5. Drift compensation of the baseline - a) Low baseline reset b) Threshold based sampling & adjustment

4.1   Room Modeling

In order to meet the specific requirements given in typical AAL applications the CapFloor software is able to model rooms and the location of different types of capacitive floor systems within those rooms. Currently there are two different types of capacitive systems supported - *floor* - that is based on the CapFloor mats introduced earlier and *smallfloor* - based on a single capacitive sensor that is able to distinguish between occupation and non-occupation of a certain area, typically realized using a small mat with a single wire connected to a sensor. These do not support localization on the mat itself and it is assumed that a person on those is standing in the middle. Another supported item are areas-of-interest (AOIs). They are specific regions within the room that are uniquely identifiable and may provide additional events within the localization scenario, e.g. triggering an event when a person enters or leaves a room. The rooms are modeled using a simple XML schema as shown below, supporting rectangular rooms with various *floors* and *smallfloors*, as well as random AOIs. All The rotation parameter for *floors* is used to identify their relative orientation to the room that is used to register localization results to global coordinates.

```
<room>
    <roomsize>1140,600</roomsize>
    <floor>
         <origin>830,40</origin>
         <size>250,250</size>
         <rotation>0</rotation>
         <id>1</id>
    </floor>
    <smallfloor>
         <origin>915,512</origin>
         <size>60,60</size>
         <id>1</id>
    </smallfloor>

    <aoi>
         <origin>915,512</origin>
         <size>60,60</size>
         <name>AOI 1</name>
    </aoi>
</room>
```

4.2   Visualization

The user interface for our CapFloor system is visualizing the modeled room, localization results and debug information, such as raw sensor data. The located

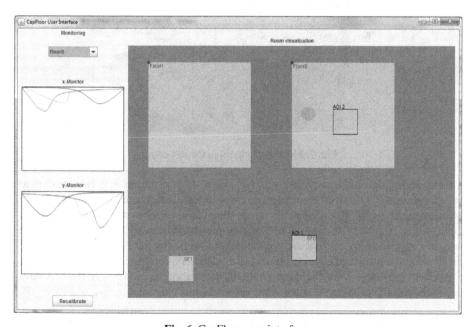

Fig. 6. CapFloor user interface

person is visualized as green dot, with smallfloors (SF), floors and AOIs shown in the right part of the screen. The left part is displaying the debug information of a single floor or smallfloor. It is possible to switch between all attached devices and visualize the location of more than one person.

5   EvAAL Competition

We participated with the CapFloor system at the 2011 EvAAL[6] indoor localization out of competition due to an unresolved IPR situation that prevented publication of technical details at this point in time.

The CapFloor system was unique in the competition as only floor-based system. An additional disadvantage was the lack of sufficient hardware to equip the whole test site. Therefore it was not possible to record all conceivable movement paths.

Fig. 7. Floor mats placed in the test area

Considering that the testing site was fully furnished, resulting in a complex setup and therefore the system did not perform well in installation complexity. This is an inherent issue with floor-based systems that has to be considered in actual applications. A factory-version would rely on pre-manufactured sets of foils that can be easily applied to rooms that are empty and placed below the floor covering. While installation in a furnished room is possible it is also very complex.

Another challenge was the large size of the testing area. Our system requires electronics to be placed on the sides of the mats which is only unobtrusive when they are

---

[6] http://evaal.aaloa.org/

adjacent to a well which is not always possible in large open spaces, such as the EvAAL test area. A different approach to hide the electronics would be required in those areas.

The system precision and availability could not be fully tested due to the lack of hardware mentioned earlier. Localization precision on the fully equipped floors was satisfactory and in the range of 50 cm. The EvAAL competition resulted in valuable feedback on our system that we can use to improve future versions of the system.

6   Conclusion and Limitations

We have introduced a flexible floor-based indoor localization system based on capacitive sensing that is specifically designed to detect position and potential falls of users in a home environment. The focus was on creating a system that is precise enough for the desired tasks, while remaining affordable and easily maintainable. Other available solutions offer more precision but are often technically complex, thus requiring extensive hardware installation that are not suited for all environments.

However this focus is leading to some limitations. The system is currently not viable for large empty spaces, due to a limited maximum mat size and sensors that have to be placed at the border. Capacitive systems do provide the opportunity to install unobtrusive indoor localization system for detecting or even distinguishing multiple persons within a predetermined location while maintaining a reasonable positioning precision. The systems are easily scalable and adaptable to support systems with a higher or inferior precision by increasing or decreasing the number of attached sensors.

As future work we intend to open the currently hard-coded rule system that adapts the localization, to allow end-user configuration, as well as improving the detection of multiple persons. Furthermore we will try to improve the overall system to allow larger rooms to be equipped as well. The software will be improved to allow the modeling of more complex geometries and support other types of sensors. For the latter part a more generalized signal processing approach will have to be developed. The results of the EvAAL competition encourage us to refine our systems in terms of scalability to large areas and improved installation, e.g. using prefabricated electrode mats.

References

1. Glinsky, A.: Theremin: Ether music and espionage. University of Illinois Press (2000)
2. Wilson, T.V., Fenlon, W.: How the iPhone Works - Multi-touch systems,
   http://electronics.howstuffworks.com/iphone2.htm
3. Lion Precision: Capacitive Displacement Sensors - An Overview,
   http://www.lionprecision.com/capacitive-sensors
4. Addlesee, M.D., Jones, A.H., Livesey, F., Samaria, F.S.: The ORL Active Floor. IEEE Personal Communications 4, 35–41 (1997)
5. Lauterbach, C., Steinhage, A.: SensFloor ® - A Large-area Sensor System Based on Printed Textiles Printed Electronics. Ambient Assisted Living Congress. VDE Verlag (2009)
6. Baxter, L.K.: Capacitive Sensors. Sensors Peterborough NH. 1-17 (1996)

OwlPS: A Self-calibrated Fingerprint-Based Wi-Fi Positioning System

Matteo Cypriani, Philippe Canalda, and François Spies

FEMTO-ST — UMR CNRS 6174,
DISC Department,
University of Franche-Comté, France
{surname.name}@univ-fcomte.fr
http://www.femto-st.fr/

Abstract. Owl Positioning System (OwlPS) is an indoor positioning system based on the IEEE 802.11 radio network (Wi-Fi). Since 2004, our team OMNI develops and experiments various techniques (both from the literature and from our own work) for indoor and outdoor positioning. We mainly exploit signal strength fingerprinting and indoor propagation models, helped by information such as the building's map, the mobile's path, etc. The latest version of the system (v1.2) includes a self-calibration mechanism, that avoids the time-consuming manual fingerprinting phase and allows taking into account dynamically the changes of the environment (human, climatic, etc.) when computing the location of the mobile terminals.

1   Introduction

In order to have good positioning accuracy indoors, one can develop a system using line-of-sight methods such as light (visible or not: infrared, laser...) or ultrasound. However, if there are obstacles between the sender and the receiver, it is required to use a medium that is able to go through them, such as radio waves. All the techniques based on radio signals have a relatively bad accuracy in heterogeneous environments such as buildings, because of the many obstacles that modify the waves' characteristics due to physical phenomena such as reflection, absorption, refraction and diffraction. Much work has been conducted in the last few years to define a radio-based positioning technique which would accurately estimate the position even in such heterogeneous environments.

Two techniques are commonly used to build an indoor positioning system based on radio waves:

- propagation models, sometimes adapted for indoor environments [1,2], along with geometrical methods such as trilateration or multilateration;
- fingerprint of the signal strength (SS) in the deployment area [3].

The propagation model-based systems are very fast to deploy but the positioning accuracy is weak. The fingerprinting method is quite slow to deploy, because

S. Chessa and S. Knauth (Eds.): EvAAL 2011, CCIS 309, pp. 36–51, 2012.

it requires one to build a cartography of the SS in the deployment area before localising mobile terminals; however, the positioning accuracy can be quite good, depending on the building complexity, the fingerprint meshing and the positioning function.

We chose to work mainly with fingerprinting-based methods, which give good results. The weak point of these approaches is the duration of the repository construction, but it seems also to be the easiest task to automate; we propose such an automation method in Section 2.4.

This paper is organised as follows: Section 2 presents the OwlPS platform in detail, then we briefly explain the deployment made at the CIAmI Living Lab during the EvAAL contest in Section 3; in Section 4 we present and discuss the results obtained after the competition.

2   The OwlPS Platform

Owl Positioning System is a Wi-Fi-based, infrastructure-centred[1] positioning system developed at the University of Franche-Comté, which implements several positioning algorithms and techniques. We first present its architecture and its deployment process, then the positioning algorithms implemented, and finally an explanation of the self-calibration mechanism.

2.1   Architecture

The OwlPS architecture, summarised in Fig. 1, is composed of several elements:

- **Mobile terminals**, such as laptops, PDAs, cell phones, hand-held game consoles, etc., which are equipped with Wi-Fi cards. These run the *owlps-client* software.
- **Access points** (APs), which capture the frames of the Wi-Fi network in order to receive any positioning request transmitted by the mobiles. These run the *owlps-listener* software, which uses the *pcap* library to capture the IEEE 802.11 frames. The SS values are extracted from the *Radiotap* [4] header of each frame, therefore the network interface's driver must support *Radiotap*[2]. It is possible to have as many APs as desired: as long as they are only listening to the radio network, they do not cause any interference.
- **The aggregation server**, to which the APs forward the captured positioning requests; its task is to gather and format these requests. It runs the *owlps-aggregator* software.

---

[1] In an infrastructure-centred architecture, the elements of the infrastructure do the measurements and compute the positions of the mobile terminals, as opposed to a mobile-centred architecture in which the mobile terminals measure and compute their own positions.

[2] On Linux, only a few drivers such as *ipw2200* or *MadWifi* used to support *Radiotap*, but nowadays, thanks to the new mac80211 infrastructure of the Linux kernel, more and more drivers are *Radiotap*-enabled [5].

– **The positioning server** (or computation server), which computes the position of each mobile from the information forwarded by the aggregation server, thanks to the *owlps-positioner* software.

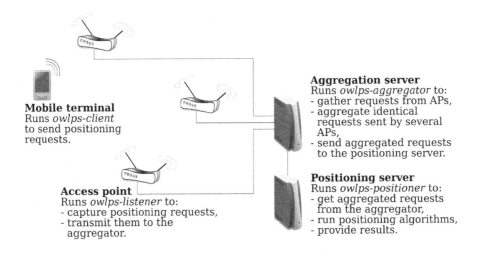

Fig. 1. Hardware and software architecture of OwlPS

All the modules are implemented in C, except *owlps-positioner*, which is written in C++. The system is designed and tested on GNU/Linux-based platforms[3]. The *owlps-client* module is not mandatory, it can be replaced (for instance on Java-based cell phones) by any software able to send a UDP packet following the adequate data format.

Of course, a single machine can run several software modules; in general the aggregation and computation modules are installed on the same host. Except for *owlps-positioner*, the memory footprint of the modules is low enough to run on most embedded hardware[4]. The hardware requirements of *owlps-positioner* depend on the number of mobiles and APs, and on the positioning algorithm selected. With a low workload (e.g. one mobile and six APs), it can run on a low-end PC without difficulty.

With a high number of capture APs, it is possible to have more than one aggregation server, each group of APs being configured to send the captured

---

[3] The *owlps-client* and *owlps-aggregator* modules also build on BSD platforms. Some parts of the network-related code of *owlps-listener* are Linux-specific, so it would require a few adaptations to work on another operating system. *owlps-positioner* builds on any UNIX-like platform with GCC 4.4 or later and the Boost libraries.

[4] Around 27MB of virtual size (1MB of resident memory) for *owlps-aggregator* and 2.7MB (1.2MB resident) for *owlps-listener*.

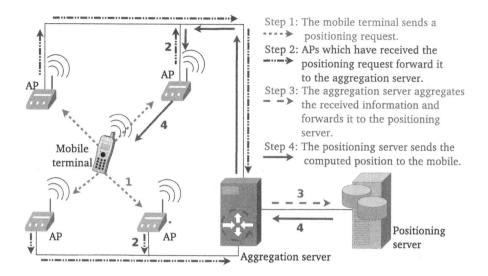

Fig. 2. Four-step process of the mobile's position resolution

positioning requests to a given aggregation server. However, it is currently not possible to have more than one positioning server in a single deployment area.

Fig. 2 summarises the four steps of the mobile's position resolution:

1. The mobile submits a positioning request to the infrastructure. This request consists of a group of identical UDP packets containing the local time on the mobile terminal; when used to calibrate the system, it also contains the current coordinates of the mobile. Fig. 3 describes the binary format of the request packet.
2. Each AP capturing the positioning request extracts the corresponding SS. Then it transmits to the aggregation server a UDP packet containing the received mobile information, the received SS, the timestamp of reception on the AP, and the mobile and AP MAC addresses.
3. The aggregation server receives the positioning requests forwarded by the APs. It gathers those corresponding to the same couple {mobile MAC address, request timestamp} and forwards them to the positioning server.
4. The positioning server analyses the information received from the aggregation server and computes the mobile's position; the result is then sent to the mobile, or processed in another way. Fig. 4 shows the various ways the positioning server can provide the computed position to a user or another software module.

2.2   Deployment

The deployment of the system is pretty straightforward, and includes the following steps:

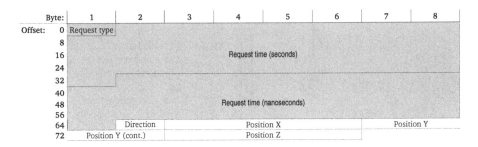

Fig. 3. Binary format of a positioning/calibration request's packet sent by the mobile, as of OwlPS 1.2. The grey fields are always present; they correspond to a positioning request (65 bytes). If the packet contains all the fields, it is a calibration request (78 bytes). All the fields must be encoded in the network's endianess (big endian).

1. Deployment of the APs into the area. They must be able to communicate with the aggregation server, either through a wired or wireless network.
2. Description of the hardware characteristics in the configuration files of the positioning server: antenna gain, transmitted power, operating radio frequency, coordinates of the fixed elements.
3. Description of the size and topology of the deployment area – optional, depending on the algorithm used.
4. Manual off-line calibration (fingerprinting) – only if self-calibration is not to be used (see Section 2.4).

2.3   Implemented Positioning Algorithms

When running the system, one must also choose at least one positioning algorithm amongst those implemented in the positioning server. The algorithms implemented in OwlPS 0.8 were described briefly and compared in [6]. Here is a quick summary of the algorithms implemented in OwlPS 1.2:

- Nearest-neighbour in Signal Strength (NSS), based on RADAR [3], which is a simple cartography-based algorithm.
- Trilateration using the propagation formula proposed by Interlink Networks in [1].
- Trilateration using the FBCM [2,7] (*Friis-Based Calibrated Model*), which adapts the propagation formula to better match the deployment area's characteristics, thanks to a minimal calibration.
- Basic FRBHM [8,7,9] (*FBCM and Reference-Based Hybrid Model*), that is a combination of the NSS and the FBCM which allows to adapt dynamically the propagation formula to the characteristics of the room where the mobile terminal is supposed to be.

Since recent work has been mostly centred on the self-calibration, the support for the Viterbi-enabled algorithms (NSS with Viterbi-like [10], Discrete and Continuous FRBHM [7,9]) was dropped as of OwlPS 1.0.

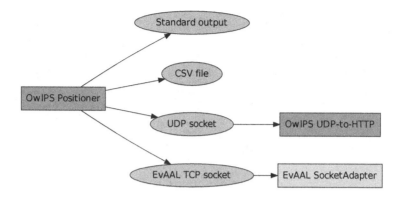

Fig. 4. Output formats supported by OwlPS Positioner v1.2, including the output developed for the EvAAL contest to connect with the `SocketAdapter` program provided by the organisers. The OwlPS UDP-to-HTTP module is a minimalist HTTP server that takes as input the results provided by the positioning server on a UDP socket, and provides the last position of each mobile request; we use this module to develop a Javascript monitoring program based on Google Maps.

2.4   Self-calibration

The OwlPS 1.2 release implements a self-calibration (or auto-calibration) mechanism that allows the system to be operational within a few minutes after its deployment. Since the self-calibration is a continuous process, it also guarantees that the system is aware of the modifications that occur in the radio environment.

For instance, if the number of people present in the building changes, if those people move within the building, if furniture is moved, if the weather changes, etc., the system will take into account the changes in order to maintain accuracy. On the other hand, with static calibration, the positioning error can raise dramatically if the environment changes. Moreover, the auto-calibration process is quick enough to allow the system to be aware of the short term modifications of the environment, for example a door that is opened or closed, someone walking through a corridor, etc.

When self-calibration is activated, the aggregation server sends the APs regular round robin orders to transmit an auto-calibration request. When receiving such an order, an AP transmits a positioning request, as if it were a mobile terminal, which will be intercepted by the other APs. The request is then processed the usual way: it is transmitted by the APs to the aggregation server and, once aggregated, to the positioning server.

The positioning server is then able to build a matrix S of the SS received by each AP of index j from each AP of index i. If we note $s_{Tx,Rx}$ the strength of a signal from a transmitter Tx to a receiver Rx, and n the number of deployed APs, the matrix S is defined as:

$$\forall i, j \in \mathbb{N}, i \neq j, i \leq n, j \leq n : S_{i,j} = s_{AP_i, AP_j} \tag{1}$$

An example of such a matrix is given in Fig. 5, for four APs.

Tx / Rx	$\mathbf{AP_A}$	$\mathbf{AP_B}$	$\mathbf{AP_C}$	$\mathbf{AP_D}$
$\mathbf{AP_A}$		-21	-60	-51
$\mathbf{AP_B}$	-23		-52	-73
$\mathbf{AP_C}$	-64	-55		-17
$\mathbf{AP_D}$	-49	-70	-19	

Fig. 5. Sample matrix of the SS received by each AP from each other, in dBm. As shown, the signal is not necessarily symmetrical, i.e. the SS received by AP_A from AP_B can be different than the SS received by AP_B from AP_A.

From the APs' matrix S, and the APs' description file (containing their coordinates and hardware characteristics, see Section 2.2), the system builds a geographical matrix, called G. Each element (i, j) of this matrix represents a spatial coordinate (x, y) of the deployment area and contains an extrapolation of the real SS values of S, that is the SS received from a virtual mobile terminal M located in (x, y) by each of the APs:

$$G_{i,j} = \{s_{M,AP_1}; s_{M,AP_2}; \ldots; s_{M,AP_n}\} \tag{2}$$

Note that x and y are the geographical coordinates (real numbers) of the virtual mobile M, but this position is stored in the matrix as the element (i, j) (i and j are integers). Fig. 6 gives an example of a geographical matrix.

As stated above, to create the element (i, j) of the matrix G, the positioning server will generate one SS per AP. To generate the SS received by AP_A from M, it first chooses, amongst all the other APs, the two that have the more acute angles with the coordinates of AP_A and M. In Fig. 7, the coordinates of the APs and virtual mobile are the following:

- AP_A: $(1, 10)$,
- AP_B: $(7, 10)$,
- AP_C: $(1, 1)$,
- AP_D: $(7, 1)$,
- M: $(6, 8)$.

Thus, the angles formed by M, AP_A, and the other APs are the following (in the angle notations, we shorten AP_X to X):

Fig. 6. Sample geographical matrix of the deployment area, with four APs in the corners. Each element of the matrix represents a geographical coordinate in the area. The physical distance between two elements, in horizontal and vertical axis, is set by the administrator when the system is deployed, depending of the area's topology. For the sake of clarity, we will consider here that two elements are separated by a distance of 1 m both horizontally and vertically, but this distance can be set independently in each axis.

- $\widehat{MAB} \simeq 22°$
- $\widehat{MAC} \simeq 68°$
- $\widehat{MAD} \simeq 34°$

Here we have $\widehat{MAB} < \widehat{MAD} < \widehat{MAC}$, therefore the two nearest APs in angle are AP_B and AP_D.

A weight is then attributed to the two selected APs: the one with the most acute angle will receive a higher weighting in the computation of the SS. The reference angle $\widehat{BAD}$ is the sum of $\widehat{MAB}$ and $\widehat{MAD}$, which equals 56°. $\widehat{MAD}$ (34°) is approximately 61% of 56°, therefore we attribute a weight $W_B = 61\%$ to AP_B, and AP_D is given a weight $W_D = 100 - 61 = 39\%$.

Once the two reference APs are selected and weighted, the SS can be computed. The principle is to evaluate the quality of the link between the considered

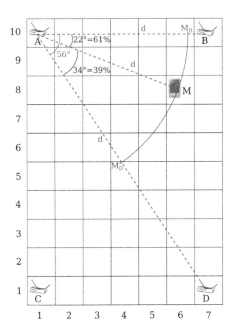

Fig. 7. Selection and weighting of the reference APs to compute the SS received by AP_A from the virtual mobile M

AP (AP_A in our example) and the reference APs (AP_B and AP_D), and to use the weights to estimate the quality of the link between AP_A and M. To evaluate the link quality, the Friis transmission equation is used. The base equation in dBm is shown in Equation 3 (the losses at the receiver and transmitter are ignored); we then demonstrate that we can write the equation in such a way that the Friis index N is computed in function of the other parameters (Equation 5).

$$Pr = Pt + Gt + Gr + 20 \log \lambda - 20 \log (4\pi) - 10 \, N \log d \qquad (3)$$
$$10 \, N \log d = Pt + Gt + Gr - Pr + 20 \log \lambda - 20 \log (4\pi) \qquad (4)$$
$$N = \frac{Pt + Gt + Gr - Pr + 20 \log \lambda - 20 \log (4\pi)}{10 \log d} \qquad (5)$$

Where:

- Pr: power gathered on the reception antenna (dBm);
- Pt: power sent to the transmission antenna (dBm);
- Gr, Gt: reception and transmission antennas' gains (dBi);
- d: distance travelled (metres);
- λ: wavelength (metres);
- N: Friis index (also called "path loss exponent").

Let d the distance between the considered AP (AP_A) and M. Let M_X a virtual mobile located at a distance d from AP_A, in the direction of AP_X. We use Equation 5 to compute the Friis index N_B, respectively N_D, for the link $AP_B \rightarrow AP_A$, respectively $AP_D \rightarrow AP_A$. As stated in the section 2.2, we already know, from the file describing the APs' hardware, the parameters Pt, Gr, Gt, and λ[5]; the distance d between the two APs is computed thanks to their coordinates, declared in the same configuration file, and Pr is the SS received by AP_A from the other AP, read from the matrix S.

Then, thanks to Equation 3, we compute the SS that would be received by AP_A from M_B, respectively M_D, using the Friis index N_B, respectively N_D. The final SS for M as received by AP_A is the mean of the SS of M_B and M_D, weighted according to the previously computed weights of AP_B (W_B) and AP_D (W_D):

$$SS_M = \frac{SS_{M_B} \times W_B}{100} + \frac{SS_{M_D} \times W_D}{100} \qquad (6)$$

The same process is repeated to generate the SS for each other AP at this position (in our example: AP_B, AP_C and AP_D). Once a SS has been generated for each AP, the coordinates of M are updated and the next element of the matrix G is created. In the end, G is filled with generated "calibration measurements", that can be used by algorithms like the NSS, as a real (manual) calibration would be used. Fig. 8 summarises the auto-calibration process.

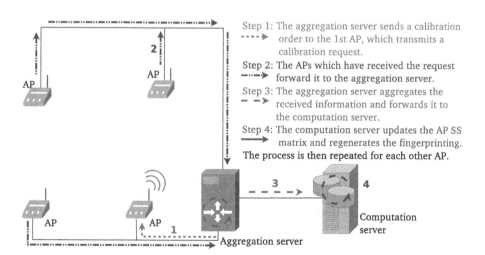

Step 1: The aggregation server sends a calibration order to the 1st AP, which transmits a calibration request.

Step 2: The APs which have received the request forward it to the aggregation server.

Step 3: The aggregation server aggregates the received information and forwards it to the computation server.

Step 4: The computation server updates the AP SS matrix and regenerates the fingerprinting. The process is then repeated for each other AP.

Fig. 8. Summary of the auto-calibration process

---

[5] The wavelength λ is computed from the propagation speed of the radio signal (we use the speed of light in vacuum, c), and its frequency f: $\lambda = \frac{c}{f}$.

3   Deployment at the CIAmI Living Lab

We describe in this section the deployment of OwlPS at the CIAmI Living Lab in Valencia, during the EvAAL competition. We deployed four Wi-Fi APs (Fonera 2.0[6] running the embedded Linux distribution *OpenWrt*), one in each corner of the evaluation area (see Fig. 9). The APs include a *Radiotap*-enabled Atheros Wi-Fi chipset, configured with the *MadWifi* tools [11].

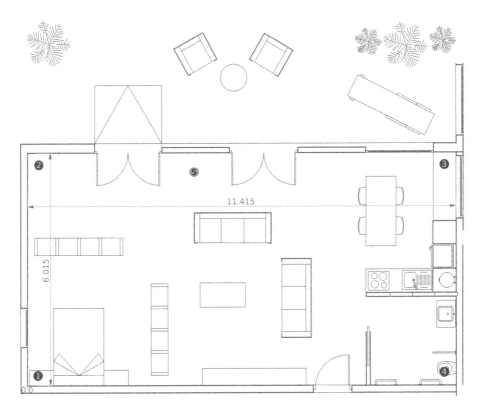

Fig. 9. Plan of the CIAmI Living Lab, with the four Foneras (blue numbered circles) deployed in each corner of the area: (1) 0.30,0.30; (2) 0.30,5.70; (3) 11.11,5.70; (4) 11.11,0.30. The server (positioning and aggregation) is represented by the green "S" circle (approximate position: 4.50,5.50).

The aggregation and positioning software modules are both installed on a Lenovo Thinkpad X200[7] running Debian GNU/Linux. The `SocketAdapter` program provided by the organisers is used to send the results to the EvAAL evaluation software. The located device is another Fonera, powered by a small battery.

---

[6] Atheros AR2315 running at 180 MHz, 32 MB RAM, 8 MB storage.
[7] Intel Core 2 Duo P8400 running at 2.26 GHz, 2 GB RAM.

All the modules communicate through an IEEE 802.11 ad-hoc network; this is possible because the Wi-Fi interfaces of the APs support running several modes (here ad-hoc and monitor) simultaneously. If the Wi-Fi interfaces were single-mode only, we would have needed to use the wired (Ethernet) network, or to add a second Wi-Fi interface to the APs[8].

The self-calibration is activated, with one auto-calibration request every 320 ms, i.e. each AP sends a request every 1280 ms. The positioning server computes the results using the NSS algorithm.

4   Competition Results' Discussion

The scores obtained by OwlPS during the EvAAL 2011 contest are given in Table 1.

Table 1. Scores obtained by OwlPS and average of the scores of the six competitors. As a reminder, the EvAAL scores range from 0 to 10.

Criterion	OwlPS	Average
Accuracy	1.3653	4.2311
Availability	9.4337	6.5147
Installation complexity	8.4733	5.8822
User acceptance	6.5	6.2083
Integrability in AAL	1	5.5833
Final score	4.85	5.0067

Undoubtedly, the main strengths of OwlPS are its high positioning rate and its quick deployment procedure, hence the scores in the *availability* and *installation complexity* criteria. There is not much to say about the availability of the system; the maximum score was not reached most likely because of a few packet losses, or maybe some desynchronisations between OwlPS and the evaluation system.

The initial deployment of the system in the living lab took only 7 minutes with one single operator, which would have allowed a score of 10 in *installation complexity*. Unfortunately, a software bug appeared in the first run of the evaluation, causing the results provided by the positioning server to be completely aberrant. Patching the software to fix the bug took approximately 10 more minutes, which of course were added to the deployment time, for a total of about 17 minutes, therefore the score was lowered.

OwlPS requires the person being localised to carry a Wi-Fi-enabled device. During the competition, this device was a Wi-Fi router with a belt clip, powered by a small battery. In a real-life deployment, a device such as a smartphone would be used, which has been judged quite acceptable by the evaluation committee. The drawback of this system is that it requires several APs to be deployed across

---

[8] The Fonera 2.0 has a USB port, in which we could plug an additional USB Wi-Fi interface.

the user's house, but this has not be seen as a major drawback. The score of *user acceptance* obtained is just above average.

The two serious flaws of OwlPS are its *accuracy* and its *integrability*. OwlPS is an experimental research project, and is mainly developed by only one programmer; since it is not a commercial product, only what is strictly necessary from a research support point of view is developed. Therefore, it does not conform with most of the criteria defined by the organisers for the *integrability in AAL*.

Monitoring. There is no pre-made monitoring tool. It would be possible (and actually quite easy) to use well-known monitoring tools such as Nagios, deploying SNMP agents on the APs and servers. However, it is true that it it not a turnkey solution, and a monitoring configuration could be provided to help the system administrator.

Documentation. The OwlPS source code is essentially self-documented; in the positioning server code, Doxygen-style comments are used to allow the generation of a documentation in a more readable format (HTML, LaTeX, man pages, etc.). A rather complete user documentation exists for OwlPS 0.8 [12] (in French), but it is not totally up-to-date with OwlPS 1.2.

External library. There is no software library allowing one to easily receive and interpret the positioning results in an external program. However, the positioning server can provide the results in several ways (as shown in Fig. 4), and it is quite easy to add new output formats; as an example, the code of the `OutputTCPSocketEvaal` C++ class added in the positioning server to participate in the contest is only 130 (real) lines long. Moreover, the CSV format used in the CSV and UDP outputs can be easily parsed with any programming language. We plan to add the support of XML for the output, so that it would be even easier to implement a parser, thanks to an XML schema.

Open Source. Finally, the OwlPS code is not public; it was planned to release it under a free software license before the summer of 2011 (i.e. before the competition), but the process is currently on hold since we are engaged in a technology transfer program.

The *accuracy* score is computed by averaging the scores of the two phases of the evaluation.

Phase 1: the positioning system has to guess the area of interest (AOI) where the user is standing; OwlPS guessed correctly in 27.31% of the cases, which gives a score of 2.731 (see Table 2).

Phase 2: the user goes through a "random" path, and the system outputs an estimation of its position in real time, the evaluation criterion being the euclidean distance error of the estimated position; for OwlPS, the global 75th percentile of error is above 4 metres, which gives a score of 0 (see Table 3).

Table 2. *Accuracy results for the phase 1 (areas of interest).* Number of times the AOI guessed by OwlPS Positioner matches or does not match the AOI where the user is.

Matches	Misses	Total
222	591	813
27.31%	72.69%	100%

Table 3. *Accuracy results for the phase 2 (random path).* Mean error (in metres), standard deviation and 75th percentile for the three routes of the second test of the phase 2. For each route, the first two column show the error in X and Y, and the third column the euclidean distance in the plan. The "Global" columns are for all the values in the three routes taken together.

	Route 1			Route 2			Route 3			Global		
	X err.	Y err.	Err.	X err.	Y err.	Err.	X err.	Y err.	Err.	X err.	Y err.	Err.
Mean	2.23	2.58	3.63	3.61	1.03	3.94	2.56	1.85	3.43	2.95	1.65	3.70
Std.	1.58	1.29	1.62	2.22	1.13	2.19	1.78	1.37	1.80	2.04	1.39	1.96
75th	2.63	3.84	4.63	5.22	1.05	5.22	3.71	3.41	4.83	3.76	2.98	4.89

If the accuracy of OwlPS is far from perfect, we can say that such results make the system pretty usable in most indoor positioning scenarios. With a mean error below 4 metres, and a 75th percentile of error below 5 metres, the room in which the user is can be determined without error in most cases. In addition, the standard deviation is relatively low, with a maximum error, all three routes taken together, of 9.44 metres. It is true however that this precision is not sufficient in scenarios such as activity recognition, in which the system needs to estimate the position with a precision of at least one metre, to be able to determine in which area of a room the user is and what he is likely to do; an estimation of the user's orientation would also help in such scenarios.

5   Conclusion

In this paper, we presented the main features of OwlPS, our Wi-Fi-based, infrastructure-centred, indoor positioning system. Its most interesting features include a scalable and flexible architecture, the use of standard and low-cost hardware, and above all a fast deployment and a low cost of maintenance thanks to its self-calibration mechanism.

The positioning software module is designed to be modular, so it is easy to implement additional positioning techniques, output formats, etc. It is also able to generate results for several positioning algorithms from the same input data, so it is really simple to compare objectively the results.

With a final score of 4.85, OwlPS is just below the average of the EvAAL competitors. There is a huge progression margin in the *integrability* and *accuracy* criteria. The former would require some work to make the system more turnkey: new output formats, software packages to ease the installation, comprehensive documentation to help the administrator during configuration, tools to monitor the infrastructure devices, etc.

We identified that the accuracy problem comes from the similarity algorithm of the nearest neighbour function. Indeed, during the positioning phase the positioning server chooses in the SS cartography the point that is the most similar to the current SS measurement from the mobile terminal. But it often happens that several points of the cartography are considered as similar, even though their geographical coordinates are far from each other. We are currently working on improving this function, by introducing new similarity algorithms based on probabilities.

However, it is to be noted that the self-calibration mechanism fulfils its goal, which is to allow a very quick deployment of the system without degrading significantly the accuracy and the positioning rate. This is highlighted by the good scores obtained in the *installation complexity* and *availability* criteria.

In the current and former deployments of OwlPS, we set up the APs so that they form a convex polygon, in which the mobile terminals are supposed to be most of the time. This is an intuitive way to deploy, but it is not proven to be the best choice. Ongoing work include optimisation of both the Wi-Fi coverage offered to the mobile terminals and the positioning accuracy.

Future work will also bear scalability improvements, for example by allowing several positioning servers to be used in a single deployment, or limiting the network traffic.

References

1. Interlink Networks, Inc.: A practical approach to identifying and tracking unauthorized 802.11 cards and access points. Technical report (2002)
2. Lassabe, F., Baala, O., Canalda, P., Chatonnay, P., Spies, F.: A Friis-based calibrated model for WiFi terminals positioning. In: Proceedings of IEEE Int. Symp. on a World of Wireless, Mobile and Multimedia Networks, Taormina, Italy, pp. 382–387 (June 2005)
3. Bahl, P., Padmanabhan, V.N.: RADAR: An in-building RF-based user location and tracking system. In: INFOCOM (2), pp. 775–784 (2000)
4. Radiotap website, `http://www.radiotap.org/`
5. Radiotap on Linux Wireless website,
   `http://linuxwireless.org/en/developers/Documentation/radiotap`
6. Cypriani, M., Lassabe, F., Canalda, P., Spies, F.: Open Wireless Positionning System: a Wi-Fi-based indoor positionning system. In: VTC-fall 2009, 70th IEEE Vehicular Technologie Conference, Anchorage, Alaska. IEEE Vehicular Technology Society (September 2009)
7. Lassabe, F., Canalda, P., Chatonnay, P., Spies, F.: Indoor Wi-Fi positioning: Techniques and systems. Annals of Telecommunications 64(9/10), 651–664 (2009)
8. Lassabe, F., Charlet, D., Canalda, P., Chatonnay, P., Spies, F.: Refining WiFi indoor positionning renders pertinent deploying location-based multimedia guide. In: Procs of IEEE 20th Int. Conf. on Advanced Information Networking and Applications, Vienna, Austria, vol. 2, pp. 126–130 (2006)

9. Cypriani, M., Canalda, P., Lassabe, F., Spies, F.: Wi-Fi-based indoor positioning: Basic techniques, hybrid algorithms and open software platform. In: Mautz, R., Kunz, M., Ingensand, H. (eds.) IPIN 2010, IEEE Int. Conf. on Indoor Positioning and Indoor Navigation, Session WLAN RSS (Signal Strength Based Methods), Fingerprinting, ETH Zurich, Campus Science City (Hoenggerberg), Switzerland, pp. 116–125 (September 2010)
10. Bahl, P., Balachandran, A., Padmanabhan, V.: Enhancements to the RADAR user location and tracking system. Technical report, Microsoft Research (February 2000)
11. MadWifi website, http://www.madwifi-project.org/
12. Cypriani, M., Canalda, P., Zirari, S., Lassabe, F., Spies, F.: Open Wireless Positioning System, version 0.8. Technical Report RT2008-02, LIFC - Laboratoire d'Informatique de l'Université de Franche Comté (December 2008)

The iLoc Ultrasound Indoor Localization System at the EvAAL 2011 Competition

Stefan Knauth[1], Lukas Kaufmann[2], Christian Jost[2],
Rolf Kistler[2], and Alexander Klapproth[2]

[1] Stuttgart University of Applied Sciences - HFT Stuttgart
Schellingstr. 24, D-70174 Stuttgart, Germany
stefan.knauth@hft-stuttgart.de
[2] Lucerne University of Applied Sciences - iHomeLab
Technikumstr. 21, CH-6048 Horw, Switzerland
info@iHomeLab.ch

Abstract. iLoc is an ultrasound ranging based indoor localization system which is deployed at the iHomeLab laboratory. For example, the system can be used for visitor tracking: Visitors get an electronic name badge comprising an ultrasound transmitter. This badge can be localized with an average accuracy of less than 10 cm deviation in its spatial position, by means of reference nodes distributed in the lab rooms. Depending on the position update rate, a small battery may suffice for several month of tag operation. Other advantages when compared to existing ultrasound ranging systems (like CRICKET, CALMARI, BAT) are for example the simple deployment with its 2 wire "IPoK" bus system. In this paper we report on the system itself and on the participating of iLoc at the first EvAAL indoor localization competition.

Keywords: Real-Time Locating Systems, Indoor Localization, Ultrasound, Ambient Assisted Living, Wireless Sensor Networks.

1 Introduction

Ultrasound time-of-flight measurement is a proven technology for indoor ranging and has already been successfully applied to indoor localization systems in the past. Prominent ultrasound based localization projects are for example the CRICKET, CALAMARI and BAT systems ([1–3]). They provide high and reliable accuracy, achieved with moderate effort. The known ultrasound systems are now some years old and the capabilities of embedded systems have evolved considerably since that time. The newly developed iLoc system takes advantage of developments among others in energy consumption, hardware size, cost, deployment effort and accuracy.

The iLoc ultrasound ranging based indoor localization system (Fig. 1) comprises badges (name tags), detector nodes and a position server, as well as network infrastructure. The name tags (Fig. 4) are equipped with a microcontroller, a radio transceiver and an ultrasound transmitter. They emit ultrasound pulses

S. Chessa and S. Knauth (Eds.): EvAAL 2011, CCIS 309, pp. 52–64, 2012.

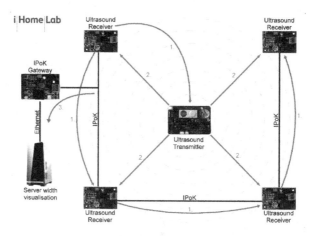

Fig. 1. Setup overview: Four reference nodes are shown. The upper left receiver sends out a synchronization signal (arrows labeled "1") by wire ("IPoK") to the other reference nodes and by radio to the mobile node (center). The mobile node emits an ultrasound pulse (arrows "2") and the reference nodes record the reception time.

at a configurable rate, for example 2 Hz, with a duration of 1 ms. These pulses are received by some of the detectors.

The detector nodes, also called reference nodes, are located at known fixed positions. They comprise a microcontroller and an ultrasound receiver as well as a 2-wire network connection to exchange data and time synchronization information. The nodes record the reception times of ultrasound bursts transmitted by the badges and transmit this information to an IP gateway via the 2 wire bus ("IPoK", [4]). A server calculates position estimates from the received data by multilateration. In the iHomeLab, the position data is used among others for visualization of visitor positions (see Fig. 3). An overview of some iLoc features is described in [5].

A more detailled system layout is sketched in fig. 2: The detector nodes are combined in groups of 10..15 devices (4 each drawn in the figure) to form one IPoK segment, linked with a "foxboard" embedded linux system to an ethernet infrastructure. Position calculation takes place at the iLoc server, from where the data is accessed by applications, for example the visualization. Synchronization and communication with the interactive badges is decoupled from the iLoc server and performed by a dedicated communication server, to increase reliability of the system.

2   Hardware

2.1   Interactive Badges

The interactive badge (Fig. 4) comprises the following hardware blocks: a CC2430 Texas Instruments microcontroller including IEEE 802.15.4 radio transceiver,

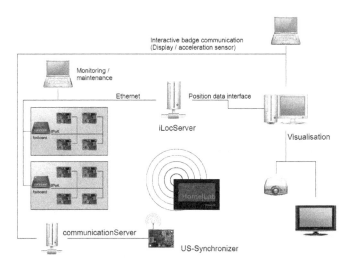

Fig. 2. System architecture: a badge emits an ultrasound burst. Reference nodes measure reception times and send them via IPoK to ethernet gateways labeled "foxboard". From there they are sent to the iLoc server. The server calculates the badge positions and offers a position data interface, which can be queried by remote applications. In the figure, a visualization client uses this interface. The badges and the receiving nodes are synchronized by the US-Synchronizer. This Synchronizer additionally implements a bidirectional communication link between the badges and interested applications, allowing sending of text to the badges LCD display and reading of acceleration- and battery state from the badge. The link is relayed by the optional communicationServer.

Fig. 3. 3D visualization of visitor positions in the iHome Lab. The positions are given as "hovering" cubes indicating the name of the badge bearer, embedded in a 3D visualization of the iHomeLab.

antenna and HF matching network, a Bosch SMB380 triaxial acceleration sensor, a charge pump chip to generate a higher voltage (20 V) to drive the 40 kHz piezoelectric ultrasound transducer, the transducer itself, the LCD unit, a rechargeable 25 mAh lithium battery as well as an inductive charging circuity. The power consumption of the badge hardware is in the range of 1..10 μW in standby mode and raises to about 50 mW in operational mode, with transition times < 1 ms. The microcontroller comprises a 32 kHz crystal-based wake up timer. The RF design and the sensor circuity is adopted from our WeBee ZigBee

Fig. 4. Name badge with IEEE802.15.4 radio transceiver, ultrasound transmitter and LCD

radio module described in [6]. The LCD carries its own controller and is connected with a serial interface. Power of the display can be switched off by the microcontroller, while the content of the display remains visible. We observed that, depending on the environmental conditions (temperature, vibrations), the display content may actually decline. Therefore a display refresh should occur from time to time, for example once a day. Display- and g-sensor related data communication is carried out between the badges and the communication server by listening and answering to synchronization radio packets which are described later.

The badges are equipped with an inductive battery charging circuity, comprising a coil (part of the PCB layout), a rectifier and overvoltage protection. The badges are charged when put into their storage box, without the need to establish any electromechanical connections, for example by plugs or contacts. The storage box comprises two charging coils operating at a frequency of 125 kHz.

2.2 Reference Nodes

The reference nodes are line-powered and minimal power consumption is not as crucial as for the badge. On the other hand, a large number of these devices have to be deployed and therefore installation and wiring shall be as easy as possible. Therefore the design is considerably different from that of the badges, notably is for example the use of a different microcontroller. The reference nodes comprise a Freescale HCS08GB60 Microcontroller.

For communication between the nodes we chose "IPoK" (IP over Klingeldraht), a protocol developed by us for easy networking of small (in size and cost) embedded devices. The idea behind IPoK is to use a 2 wire multipoint connection as for example RS485, and also supply power via the lines. The IPoK bus carries a 7..30 Volt supply, which is decoupled from the lines by inductors and then converted to 3.3 Volts with a DC-DC converter. The data TX signal is directly coupled in from the Microcontroller. The HCS08 series of controllers offer a 20 mA line driver for the included UART such that the controller can directly drive the line via a capacitor. When not sending, the UART line can be switched to high impedance and no external driver is necessary. For RX, the signal is AC coupled to a comparator or even easier to a pair of standard HC14 Schmitt-Triggers. This leads to a minimum hardware effort for the bus interface circuity.

3   Operation, Timing and Synchronization

The maximum detection range of the iLoc ultrasound signal is about 15 meters corresponding to a maximum ultrasound pulse "livetime" of less than 50 msec. This live time is given by the transmitter ultrasound amplitude, the sound path loss, and the receiver sensitivity, and is a consequence of the specific iLoc device parameters and the used sound frequency of 40 kHz.

There exist several design approaches for ultrasound localization systems with multiple mobile nodes. It is important to avoid ultrasound interference between the nodes (see for example [1]). One commonly used approach is to let the fixed infrastructure emit the pulses and send radio packets identifying the sending node. This has some advantages, for example privacy. The mobile node can detect its position without the system knowing that the mobile node exists. Also the number of mobile nodes is not limited in this case as they are passive. A disadvantage of this approach is that the mobile node has to listen for a certain time to radio and sound messages before being able to detect its position.

A main design goal of the iLoc system is that the mobile nodes (currently the name badges) shall consume as little energy as possible. Therefore we chose the opposite approach, using active mobile nodes and a passive detection infrastructure. The mobile nodes themselves emit the ultrasound pulse. For each node a 50 ms time slot is allocated, corresponding to the maximum lifetime of the propagating ultrasound pulse. The time needed for the position determination of n nodes is therefore $T = n \times 50\text{ms}$. A typical number of nodes in our lab is $n = 20$, so the position update rate for the nodes is 1 Hz. Other update rates are configurable, for example 10 Nodes with an update rate of 2 Hz each.

To allow the TDMA operation, the whole system is synchronized. As mentioned, the fixed nodes communicate via the "IPoK" two wire cabling. The system comprises several "IPoK" segments, each connected via ethernet to the iLoc server. Within the segments, the nodes are synchronized by data packets via IPoK. Each segment comprises a dedicated node which receives radio synchronization messages from a central time information transmitter, driven by the communication server.

The central synchronization radio signal is also used by the mobile nodes (name badges) for synchronization. To achieve a synchronization accuracy of about 50 μs, the mobile nodes need to resynchronize every 2-5 seconds. Actually the operation is as follows: The synchronization signal is sent with the slot rate, i.e. every 50 ms, containing also the number of the badge that shall send a pulse in the current slot. For $n = 20$, the nodes therefore wake up every second just prior to the moment when they expect their next synchronization signal. They listen for the synchronization packet, readjust their clock, emit their pulse and go to sleep again. The whole sequence takes about 5 ms, leading to a duty cycle of 1/200. The electric current in active mode is about 20 mA, leading to an average current of about 100 μA, at a voltage of 2.5 .. 3 V, enabling operation times of 10 days with a small lithium coin cell, and one update per second. The following table lists some operational times:

Battery type	Duty cycle	operational time
Lithium coin 25 mAh	1 sec	10 days
	10 sec	3 month
Lithium 500 mAh	1 sec	1/2 Year
	10 sec	> 2 Years
AA 2000 mAh	1 sec	2 Years

4   Deployment in the iHomeLab

Basically, 3 range measurements from 3 different reference positions allow the determination of the tag position. Given the above mentioned 15 meter iLoc maximum ultrasound range, these conditions would be fulfilled for example by deploying the reference nodes in a lattice with a spacing of about 10 meters. Practically, depending on the desired accuracy, the density of reference nodes should be much higher such that the distance to the furthermost node does not exceed approximately 5 meters. Then every point in the room is in the ultrasound range of more than 5 reference nodes, increasing the stability of the system against ultrasound interference for example by noise emitted from machinery or people. The ultrasound signal needs a line-of-sight for propagation, which can get lost by a shading caused by the body of the wearer of the tag or by other visitors in the same room. Also reflections have to be taken into account.

In the lab currently more than 70 nodes are arranged in 6 IPoK bus segments (fig. 5). Typically an emitted pulse is detected by about 5–15 receivers. Inconsistent range reports are rejected by the multilateration algorithm with a simple but computing intensive procedure: From the reported ranges for all permutations of 3 readings a position value is calculated. By stepwise removing of calculated positions lying outside of the mean value, the most probable readings are selected for the final trilateration [7].

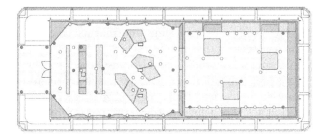

Fig. 5. Positions of the 70+ ultrasound receivers in the iHomeLab. The inner gray rectangle indicates the covered area (about $10m \times 30m$). The iHomeLab is located at Lucerne University of Applied Sciences at Campus Horw.

The deployment effort is kept at a reasonable level by using a 2 wire bus system providing power supply and communication to the nodes. Such two wire systems are commonly used for building automation purposes, and are often referred to as "fieldbus". There exist a variety of standards and vendors. As mentioned we did not opt for an existing fieldbus system but used our own implementation ("IPoK") to keep the bus interface hardware on the nodes simple.

In order to achieve a high accuracy of the system, the positions of the ultrasound receivers need to be accurately determined. Actually only a fraction of the positions have been laser measured. For the remaining positions only estimations have been entered to the database. Then the estimations have been adjusted by reference measurements: A mobile tag (name badge) was placed at a grid of known reference positions and time-of-flight results were recorded by the receivers. The position data of the reference receivers was then adjusted until the measured range values for a particular reference node matched best with the calculated distances. This fitting process was performed by minimizing the sum of the squared differences between measured range and calculated range.

Another possible automatic reference position determination solution is "leap-frogging" [8], especially feasible for temporary deployments: Here the position of some reference nodes for example at a corner of the deployment area is determined manually. Then a subsequent node is localized by the system using the already localized nodes, and so on. This mode requires the ability to use a given ultrasound transducer of a node not only as receiver, but also as transmitter. The feature is currently going to be implemented for future deployments.

5   Applications

Acceleration sensor data is used by the fall detection application: If the badge measures unusual acceleration values, it reports these values to the system. The fall detection application acquires position data from the iLoc server, analyzes the data and situation and decides whether a fall alert shall be generated. A sample of such an alert screen is shown in fig. 6. Also long term motion patterns of bearers can be recorded and analyzed to detect unusual behavior of persons

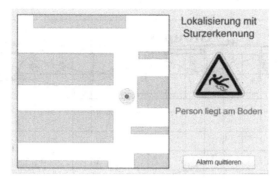

Fig. 6. Fall detection application: The name badges transmit acceleration sensor data to the system. In case of a fall, an alert is generated, indicating the location of the incident.

like changed wake up time, slower motion speed, etc. which may indicate a medical threat.

In a setup where the system is used in a hospital or a retirement home, context-relevant information may be indicated by the badges display such that a nurse nearby may immediately see relevant emergency medication or illnesses of the patient which may have to be considered in the emergency treatment. Of course, the system may also be used without display, allowing the employment of smaller tags.

Another application in the area of assistance systems is finding of assets. For example, the medicine box, telephone, or glasses may be equipped with an ultrasound tag. If the owner cannot remember where he had placed these things, he may by some modality be informed about the current position of his belongings.

6   Competition Negotiation at CIAMI Living Lab

6.1   Setup

For the competition a setup with 28 receiver nodes arranged in 3 IPoK lines has been chosen. This leads to roughly 2.5 m^2 coverage per node. It was a requirement that the system had to be installed within one hour. This ruled out the common deployment approach where first the nodes are placed and later the positions of the nodes are determined. Instead, the positions of the nodes were defined prior to the physical installation. Positions where chosen such that they lay in junctions of the lattice structure of the Living Lab ceiling (fig. 7).

This allowed physical node placing to be performed without having to use any measurement equipment like laser devices or a tape measure. The nodes were placed on certain predefined positions of the ceiling grid, by means of double-sided adhesive tape. Of course, this approach relies on a grid or other alignment structure, which is not normally given in a typical home. The three IpOK lines

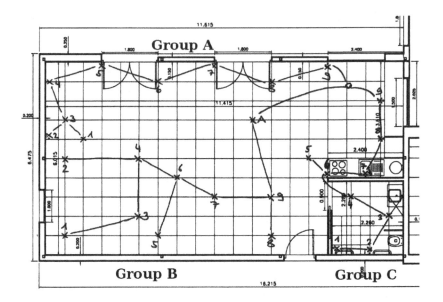

Fig. 7. Positions of the 28 iLoc receivers at CIAMI Living Lab. The nodes are arranged in 3 wiring groups, as indicated in the image.

had been wired already at our workshop such that no wiring had to be performed on site. The setup time for the system at CIAMI Living Lab was about one hour, and was mainly caused by the taping of the pre-wired nodes.

6.2   Accuracy

The score evaluation procedures were defined and published by the EvAAL technical committee, well before the competition run. We will discuss here mainly the accuracy score, which comprises a tracking run and an AOI (area of interest) detection. The rule for the tracking accuracy is to look at the individual error for each position measurement. This is the distance between the real position and the position reported by the localization system. The overall error is defined as the highest of the lower 75 percent of reported error values. From this overall error value, a score is calculated.

The obtained accuracy score for iLoc was 8.8 which means that 75 percent of the measurements were better than 80 centimeters. A typical result is shown in fig. 8. The figure indicates that the accuracy performance of the system was quite position-dependent. The walk of the test person starts in the sleeping room. Here the error is above 1 meter. After leaving the sleeping room, the track traverses the living room towards the bathroom. In this phase the deviation from the actual track is well below 50 cm, despite some outlying points which might have been induced by acoustic or electromagnetic noise. The situation changes again when entering the bathroom. Here the path in the room again shows derivations of above one meter, the final position is then detected well.

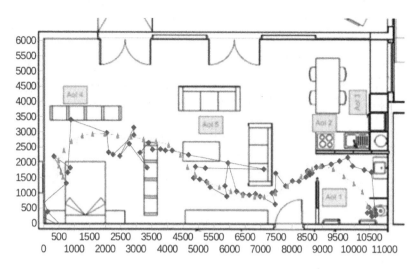

Fig. 8. Positions obtained for a specific test during the competition at CIAMI Living Lab. Bright/yellow triangles indicate real path, dark/red diamonds indicate iLoc results.

In order to detect a position value, a minimum of 3 nodes have to receive a direct ultrasound signal. If more nodes receive a signal, the quality of the position reading is increased among others by the ability to detect and ignore reflected signals [7]. The sleeping room and the bathroom were equipped with 4 receivers (fig. 7). As the badge mostly transmits in front of its bearer, it is possible that direct transmission occurs only to two receivers, degrading considerably the performance. The performance in the quite open living area was considerably better since more nodes had line-of-sight with the transmitting badge.

The score for the AOI detection is derived from the ratio "number of correct reports" divided by "total number of reports". iLoc obtained score was 71 percent, meaning that 71 percent of the measurements where assigned the correct AOI respectively "no AOI". The AOIs were squares with a size of 60 times 60 cm. Fig. 9 allows a qualitative discussion: Most of the AOIs have been detected well. Actually the final AOI positions were slightly different from those indicated in the figure, but still AOI 5 (in front of the sofa) was not detected correctly, and also AOI 6 (the right AOI in the kitchen area) was somewhat shifted. A possible reason could be a misalignment of receivers. In the case of AOI 5, the values were heavily disturbed and spread. This might be attributed to the sound produced by the metronome, which was used to synchronize the movement of the person walking on the path.

7   Results and Outlook

The iLoc indoor localization systems currently tracks for example 10 mobile nodes with a position update rate of two measurements per second per node,

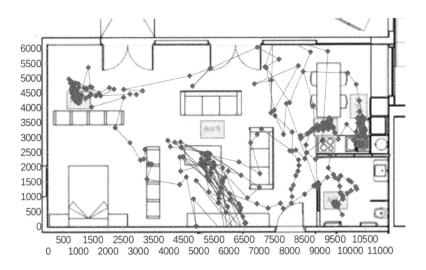

Fig. 9. Positions obtained for the AOI detection during the competition at CIAMI Living Lab

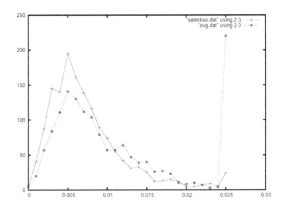

Fig. 10. Observed position error in a lab environmet after careful adjustment (not the EvAAL setup): dashed line (blue, *) indicates positions which were obtained by multilateration. Solid line (red, +) indicates positions calculated with trilateration and a selection algorithm. X-Axis: error [meters], Y-Axis: number of samples [7].

with an accuracy below 10 cm, for single measurements with no temporal averaging applied. Fig. 10 shows data from a set of about 1500 subsequent measurement cycles, with at most 8 out of 9 reference nodes reporting time stamps. The rightmost values include all measurements lying outside of the graphs X-Axis. During the recording of the observations, the sound propagation was intentionally disturbed by noise, i.e. people walking around thereby shielding the ultrasound reflectors. The high overall accuracy of the reported position values (95% within <2 cm) has been achieved by careful determination of the sound velocity and position data of the reference nodes. Under "real world" conditions, the error is typically still be well below 30 cm, provided that the alignment of the nodes has been performed with respective care.

The 2011 EvAAL competition allowed to compare the system with other competitors and technologies under identical conditions close to a real AAL scenario. We found that

- The obtained accuracy results were among the best in the competition.
- The room affiliation to bathroom, living room, sleeping room etc. was always correct.
- The installation effort was high compared to other competitors. It was still possible to set the system hardware up within 1 hour.
- User acceptance and software integration capabilities should be increased.

The results of the event strongly influenced the further development of the system. Currently the system is changed to comprise a battery powered wireless infrastructure. This, together with an automatic calibration procedure, considerably decreases installation effort. The abandonment of the wiring also increases user acceptance as the system is visually less present. The overall accuracy of the iLoc system is higher than the one obtained by the participating radio signal strength based systems. We especially propose the iLoc indoor localization system for situations where accurate positioning and tracking and an accurate room affiliation is needed in a particular AAL application.

The installation of the system is possible with moderate effort in typical indoor housing, warehouse or laboratory environments. The development includes the basic ranging electronic setup, firmware, system aspects, the timing- and multilateration algorithms, middleware and application software. Current applications of the system are visitor tracking and fall detection. The two way radio communication enables, among others, applications in the field of ambient assisted living. Long term battery operation is ensured by strict TDMA operation. The iLoc system is installed at the iHomeLab (www.iHomeLab.ch) at Lucerne University of Applied Sciences. The focus of further applications in the iHomeLab will lie in the sector of ambient assisted living.

We were glad to participate at the first EvAAL competition on Indoor Localization and experienced the EvAAL initiative with its combination of scientific workshop and real system competition as very encouraging and fruitful.

References

1. Smith, A., Balakrishnan, H., Goraczko, M., Priyantha, N.B.: Tracking Moving Devices with the Cricket Location System. In: 2nd International Conference on Mobile Systems, Applications and Services (Mobisys 2004), Boston, MA (June 2004)
2. Whitehouse, K., Jiang, F., Karlof, C., Woo, A., Culler, D.: Sensor field localization: A deployment and empirical analysis. UC Berkeley Technical Report UCB//CSD-04-1349 (April 2004)
3. Ward, A., Jones, A., Hopper, A.: A new location technique for the active office. IEEE Personal Communications 4(5), 42–47 (1997)
4. Knauth, S., Kistler, R., Jost, C., Klapproth, A.: Sarbau - an ip-fieldbus based building automation network. In: Proc. 11th IEEE Intl. Conference on Emerging Technologies and Factory Automation (ETFA 2008), Hamburg, Germany (October 2008)
5. Knauth, S., Jost, C., Klapproth, A.: iloc: a localisation system for visitor tracking and guidance. In: Proceedings of the Embedded World Conference 2009, Nuremberg, Germany (March 2009)
6. Klapproth, A., Bissig, S., Venetz, M., Knauth, S., Kaslin, D., Kistler, R.: Design of a versatile lowcost ieee802.15.4 module for long term battery operation. In: Proc. 1st European ZigBee Developers Conference - EuZDC 2007, Munich, Germany (June 2007)
7. Knauth, S., Jost, C., Klapproth, A.: Range sensor data fusion and position estimation for the iloc indoor localisation system. In: Proc. 12th IEEE Intl. Conference on Emerging Technologies and Factory Automation (ETFA 2009), Palma de Mallorca, Spain (September 2009)
8. Navarro-Serment, L., Grabowski, R., Paredis, C., Khosla, P.: Millibots. IEEE Robotics and Automation Magazine 9(4) (December 2002)

Towards a Reusable Design
of a Positioning System for AAL Environments*

Tomás Ruiz-López, Carlos Rodríguez-Domínguez,
Manuel Noguera, and José Luis Garrido

Software Engineering Department,
University of Granada,
Periodista Daniel Saucedo Aranda s/n, 18071 Granada, Spain
{tomruiz,carlosrodriguez,mnoguera,jgarrido}@ugr.es
http://lsi.ugr.es

Abstract. There exists a large diversity of decisions to be dealt with in
the design and construction of positioning systems, each of them implying different advantages and disadvantages. We present a design proposal
which aims to provide reusable and adaptable support to Location-based
Systems, through a reconfigurable positioning service composed of interoperable components. The interest of the proposal concerns the combination between different methods, algorithms and technologies to be
selected in run-time so as to take advantage of the benefits of each one
of them. The positioning system aims to use that technology which is
more beneficial taking into account the quality properties that need to
be fulfilled at a given time. For instance, the proposal enables AAL solutions to address indoor and outdoor positioning by means of the same
service switching dynamically and automatically between methods and
technologies, and combine two different methods simultaneously to improve accuracy. This research work also describe results obtained from a
competition with other proposals.

Keywords: positioning systems, SOA, radio frequency, non-functional
requirements, adaptation.

1 Introduction

Service-Oriented Architecture (SOA) is a new paradigm which aims to address
software complexity by applying a set of principles (reusability, loose coupling,
statelessness, etc.) to the creation of services, which are composed to satisfy the
system requirements. It represents a higher level step from Component-based
Design and Object-Oriented Development.

Design of services can give a high reusability to software. However, there exist scenarios where the wide variety of circumstances makes it difficult to reuse

* This research work is funded by Project P10-TIC-6600 granted by the Andalusian
Regional Government; Project 20F2/36 funded by CEI-BioTIC Granada.; and the
scholarship program FPU, granted by the Spanish Ministry of Education.

S. Chessa and S. Knauth (Eds.): EvAAL 2011, CCIS 309, pp. 65–79, 2012.

services. That is the case of services for Ambient Assisted Living (AAL) environments. The heterogeneity of environments, devices and requirements hinders the creation of highly reusable software services. Most of these services end up being built in an ad-hoc manner for the target situation, and they can only be reused if the conditions in the environment are similar.

In this paper we introduce a design for a Positioning Service, called Sherlock, which was presented at the EvAAL competition in 2011. This type of systems often use different technologies and positioning methods depending on their availability or the application requirements. They can also be deployed in different ways, which influences the architecture of the positioning system. Moreover, the requirements of this kind of systems are not static, but can change over the time. For instance, applications can require both indoor and outdoor positioning; also, different accuracy levels can be demanded from each application.

Ideally, it would be desirable to enable an adaptable and adaptive service which permits to combine different decisions with respect to the positioning methods or technologies being suitable, since the election of them has an impact on the satisfaction of the non-functional requirements expected by the end users. Exchangeability of these components raises the possibilities to build more reusable services, due to their ability to adapt themselves to uneven conditioning. Our proposal tries to address this concern by designing a service, based on interoperable components which can be reconfigured in runtime to enhance the fulfillment of quality properties.

The rest of this paper is structured as follows: section 2 introduces a design of a hybrid and adaptable Positioning Service, called Sherlock. In section 3, some experimentation results are presented. Then, in section 4, results and lessons learnt from the 1st *Evaluating AAL Systems through Competitive Benchmarking (EvAAL)* Competition are exposed. Some related work are presented in section 5, and the main conclusions drawn from this research, together with some future work, are summarized in section 6.

2 Sherlock, a Hybrid and Adaptable Positioning Service Based on Standard Technologies

In this section we are presenting a design of a positioning service, taking into consideration the main goal of this work mentioned above. The positioning service is intended to work on an SOA, and aims to be hybrid in several aspects:

- It provides indoor and outdoor positioning, using available technologies.
- It can combine several technologies in order to perform the previous task, and switch among them upon suitability.
- It can integrate different positioning algorithms and switch among them.
- It can work in the different possible architectures configurations (Figure 1) depending on the needs of the LBS which is making use of it [9].

Note that this hybridization of the system will eventually lead to the satisfaction of the non-functional requirements, as we explain in the following sections.

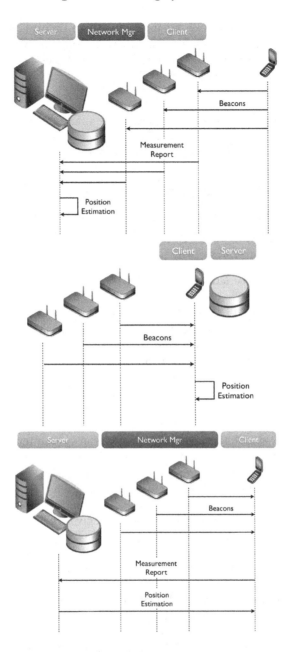

Fig. 1. Different positioning architecture settings. From top to bottom: *Network-based*, *Terminal-based* and *Terminal-assisted*.

This positioning service has been devised to work on an SOA. The rationale behind this decision is to count on a reusable, loosely coupled system to be able to provide positioning to several systems which can demand its services.

Figure 2 shows how this service can interact with a LBS in an SOA. Depending on the concrete technology we are using, different wrappers (WSDL, OWL-S or WS-BPEL, among others) based on standard technologies can be built on top of the system in order to expose the service contract.

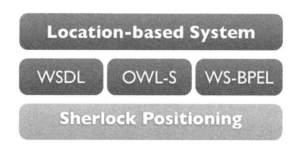

Fig. 2. SOA based interaction of an LBS and the Positioning Service

An LBS does not need to care about the details of how positioning is done or which technology the device is employing to perform that task; the positioning service makes those details transparent to the final application.

Designers of LBS only have to focus on the service contract in order to build their systems. The inner layers of the positioning service are shown in Figure 3. As depicted, a client-server architecture has been chosen for the service. In this way, the service can be distributed. The rationale behind this architectural decision is to increase the reusability of the service.

The Client-Server architecture allows to split the system into two parts: the client, which is in charge of taking measurements from the signals it receives (e.g. measuring the Received Signal Strength of a radio signal), and the server, which is responsible of computing the estimated position [12].

As shown in Figure 1, the client and the server can be deployed in different ways to adopt the three usual architectures [9]. It gives the possibility to choose one of them, or a combination, depending on the final application which is using the positioning system; therefore, the reusability of the service is enhanced since we are not coupled to a single architecture. Note that, when the client and the server are deployed separately, we need to use a middleware to communicate between them. In this case, we use BlueRose [13], which is a middleware being developed in our research group and it is oriented to context-aware applications and ubiquitous systems, but other platforms supporting communications are also available (CORBA, RMI, SOAP), since communications are encapsulated in components which can be replaced in a transparent way.

Both client and server expose a set of interfaces which are realized by their inner components. Designers of LBS do not need to know the internals of each part, just the interfaces to access the required functionality. This leads to a transparent access to the positioning service, which allows us to exchange and reconfigure components without affecting to external services using the proposed system. This is particularly helpful when the system aims to adapt to the current needs of the final applications, which typically involves addition, removal or substitution of some components to satisfy their requirements. Client and server handle the requests and choreography their inner components to perform the demanded task.

Client side of the service (figure 3) has the ability to perform measurements. It has a Sensor Manager, which is in charge of managing all the different technologies which are available. This component hides the details of the underlying technologies and their way of measurement from the rest of the system. It also allows the addition of new sensor technologies thanks to the use of interoperable components which share a common interface. GPS, WiFi or ZigBee, among others, are developed as driver components which implement this interface and provide different measurements of signal features.

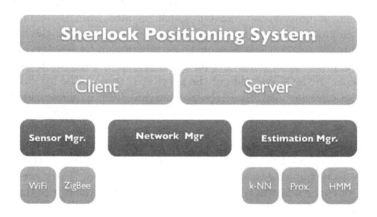

Fig. 3. Layered design for the Positioning System

Measurements are organized in a hierarchical structure. They are categorized in two levels: firstly, they are separated by the technology used to measure them; then, they are classified by the feature they measure. In this way, measurements for a certain technology can be efficiently retrieved and compared to the ones in the reference set. Moreover, this allows clients with different technologies to share the same reference set, since only the measurements with same technology are compared.

On the other hand, server side of the system is responsible of making the position estimation. Its main component is a Localizer Manager. Similar to the Sensor Manager, this component chooses the positioning methods depending on the requirements which have to be satisfied at a certain moment. It allows the installation and substitution of positioning algorithms as well, since they have to implement a common interface. k-Nearest Neighbors, Neural Networks or

Probabilistic methods are some examples of positioning methods which implement this component specification.

New technologies or positioning methods can be added and used even during runtime. This is possible thanks to the implementation of these components, as they are realized by plugins. In this way, the system is able to acquire them and work without needing to recompile or even stop its work.

Client and server can communicate by means of a middleware which hides the details of the actual way of communication or network which has been used. It hides the communication issues and can also be substituted for the most convenient option in each case, or even completely removed if the architecture does not need communications. Thus, a positioning request is served as follows. An LBS invokes this operation. It is passed to the client side of the system, which queries its driver components. These components respond with a set of measurements, which are sent to the server side, via the middleware. Server chooses which positioning methods are going to be used, and provides them with the measurements and the reference set of fingerprints in order to estimate the user's location. Then, it obtains the location which resulted from the computation, which is subsequently sent back to the LBS in order to complete the task.

There are other relevant components to be mentioned, for instance, the component that is in charge of managing the reference set of fingerprints. This component, located in the server side of the service, is responsible for storing and retrieving the reference set. Similarly to what has been explained above, this component has a well defined interface which allows us to substitute it by a more suitable one. For instance, fingerprints can be stored in a relational database. In some other cases, memory requirements can be very high, and we do not have enough storage to install a database management system; then, other ways of storage have to be implemented, like XML or plain text files. The corresponding component hides the way this components are stored from the rest of the system, and all of them are accessed in a uniform and transparent way.

We have emphasized the use of interfaces between different components in order to ensure that every interaction between components is made through these interfaces. Thanks to the use of interoperable components, different combinations of them can be included in the system to adapt it to particular circumstances, and this fact leads to a more reusable and customizable service design. Components do not know about each other and allow us to replace them in an easy way, depending on the non-functional requirements which are expected for the application under consideration at a given time. For instance:

- If indoor and outdoor positioning is required, driver components for GPS and WLAN technologies, among others, can be simultaneously included in the system.
- WLAN technology (WiFi) can typically give accuracy at room level. If more accuracy is needed, it can be combined to RFID, which can improve this requirement due to its limited range. If the cost is too high to maintain both, one of them can be removed without affecting the rest of the system.

- If the device we are using to compute the locations has strong storage limitations, we can choose to employ plain text storage. If we update the system in such a way it get more storage capabilities, this component can be replaced by a relational database manager.
- Some methods can provide better accuracy, with the drawback of needing more computation and, consequently, increasing the response time of the system specially if the amount of people using the service grows. If the responsiveness of the system has to be improved, the system can choose an algorithm which scales better and maintains an acceptable precision.
- Combination of technologies also increases robustness of the system, since we don't rely on a single technology and, after an eventual failure, it can be ignored until repaired; the system will be able too work using other available technologies meanwhile.

3   Results

The system was implemented and tested using ZigBee as a measuring technology (sensing the received signal strength, since it is easily available) and deploying it in a network-based architecture (less invasive for the user). The k-Nearest Neighbors [10] (selecting 3 and 5 neighbors) and a Proximity based technique were chosen as positioning algorithms. As for the hardware, Arduino boards [3] were used, with a XBee module plugged onto it, which is responsible for measuring the transmitted signal from the mobile unit, and a PC with another XBee receiver (the coordinator of the network), that is in charge of computing the locations. Size of the board is 6.85 cm of width and 5.33 cm of height. The coordinator is located in the Living Room, as indicated in Figure 3. The triangles represent the location of the fixed ZigBee receivers, and the crosses represent the points used to train the system. For each reference point, four measurements were taken and tagged with the corresponding location.

Tests were performed in an Ambient Assisted Living environment. Four base stations are in charge of measuring the radio signal. A mobile unit periodically transmits a signal in order to be located. The mobile unit is carried by a user (e.g. in his/her pocket) who has to be positioned.

The first test tried to compare the different accuracies of the implemented positioning methods, varying their parameters (changing the number of neighbors, selecting between Euclidean and Manhattan distance as a similarity metric). We found that the 3-NN algorithm with Euclidean distance gave accuracy greater than 90% at the room level, whereas the proximity based techniques barely reach the 50% of accuracy. The similarity criterion used was:

$$L_p = \frac{1}{N} \cdot (\sum_{i=1}^{N} |x_i - x_i'|^p)^{\frac{1}{p}} \tag{1}$$

The second test tried to compare the extrapolation capabilities of these methods. The system tried to position the mobile unit in some locations that were not

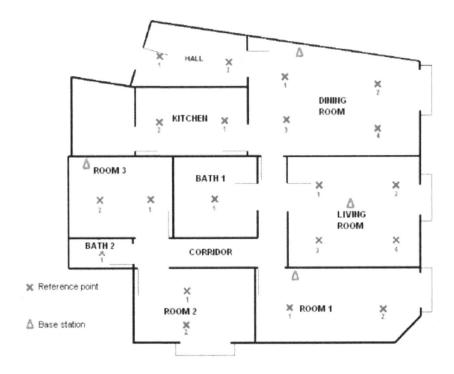

Fig. 4. Home scenario where the Positioning System was tested

present in the training set. Since symbolic locations are used, neither of them gave the actual location, but again, the 3-NN obtained an estimation which was closer to the actual position. The robustness of the service (switching down a signal transmitter) and the scalability (testing the accuracy before and after an expansion of the covered area) were also tested. In both cases, the accuracy of either method suffered degradation (less than 80% of accuracy in k-NN).

Finally, accuracy degradation along the time was tested by performing accuracy tests some weeks after the training took place, and if the accuracy degrades with the movement, by tracking a person moving through the AAL environment. In the former case, similar values to those got after the training were obtained. In the latter one, the predicted track presented wrong estimations when the person was entering a new room, which suggests the need of some software or hardware mechanism to detect when people are in transition between two rooms (e.g. just at the door).

4   The EvAAL 2011 Competition

The first *Evaluating AAL Systems through Competitive Benchmarking (EvAAL)* Competition was held between July 2011 and September 2011, in Valencia (Spain) and Lecce (Italy), respectively. The hereby presented positioning system was accepted to this competition. The first stage was carried out in the

Table 1. Comparison of the positioning method tested during the experimentation

Test	k-**Nearest Neighbors**	**Proximity-based**
Accuracy	$> 90\%$	$\sim 50\%$
Extrapolation	Obtained the closest trained location	Failed to compute an acceptable location
Robustness and Scalability	Accuracy degradation ($< 80\%$)	Accuracy degradation near the source of failure, same accuracy far from it
Time accuracy	Maintained accuracy	Maintained accuracy
Tracking	Estimation problems in borders between rooms	Unable to track with acceptable accuracy

CIAmI Living Lab in Valencia. This lab resembles an actual smart home where AAL Systems are deployed. Competitors were given 3 hours to demonstrate their systems.

First of all, the system had to be installed and deployed in the smart home. In order to quantify the installation complexity, the evaluation committee timed how long this operation lasted and how many people were involved in the installation. In the case of Sherlock, two people were needed to deploy the system. The set up consisted of 10 Arduino Uno [3], each one with an XBee Module implementing protocol 802.15.4, plus an XBeeShield, an adaptor to be able to plug the XBee Module to the Arduino board. Nine of these boards were used as base stations, whereas one of them was carried by the user and was also tracked. The chosen architecture was a Network-based architecture, where a dedicated server was in charge of obtaining the measurements from the base stations and computing the location. This server was a laptop PC which was connected to the evaluating committee's server, where results were transmitted and stored.

The deployment time was longer than expected; this was a huge disadvantage of our system since we relied on the fingerprinting technique. The required accuracy forced us to establish a very fine-grained grid were fingerprints were taken, implying a very long time to capture them.

Once the system was deployed, competitors were asked to leave the house and several tests were performed by the members of the evaluating committee. There were two kind of tests: first, systems needed to detect if the user was located at a certain area of interest (AOI) or not, and provide its corresponding symbolic location; second, a user had to be tracked through 5 different paths, providing his absolute location. These tests aimed to measure the accuracy of the system and its availability (ability to provide positioning in real-time). The performance of Sherlock in the accuracy test was poor; this was due to the fact that it has been devised to provide symbolic locations (AOI), but not absolute coordinates. Therefore, accuracy was hurt during the second part of the tests. Moreover, since the training phase during the deployment stage was badly performed, it also contributed to achieving bad results in this criterion. However, the system was able to accomplish the availability requirement with a good score, thanks to the above mentioned design decisions which optimized the computation of location estimations.

Fig. 5. Arduino boards with the XBee Modules (*left*). Laptop PC in charge of computing location estimations (*right*).

The evaluation committee allowed two opportunities to perform the same tests, taking the best marks of each ones. After that, two other evaluation criteria were checked: user acceptance and integrability in AAL systems. Both of them were evaluated through an exhaustive interview with all the members in the evaluation committee, who asked different questions regarding such aspects. For the former criterion, questions about devices which need to be carried by the users in order to be positioned, their weight, size, energy consumption, wearability or user awareness about the system, among others, were posed. In our opinion, it was an exhaustive questionnaire which made possible the evaluation of a very subjective criterion; nevertheless, we also believe that a more accurate method should be developed in order to avoid biased results among evaluations of different systems and try to obtain an evaluation method as objective as possible.

Regarding the integrability of the positioning system into other AAL systems, the evaluation committee asked different questions regarding the use of standards of the system, the existence of public documentation about the system, the existence of source libraries to integrate the system, or the existence of tools to monitor or test the positioning system, among others. Besides, competitors were asked to actually integrate their systems into the UniversAAL middleware with a twofold purpose: show the integrability of the system and broadcast the location estimations during the accuracy tests.

The integration process was presumably easy; in order to incorporate the positioning system into the UniversAAL middleware, a very simple interface needed to be implemented, providing code for three simple methods. This apparently easy task turned out to be really difficult; although we had previous experience with the programming language and the IDE (Java and Eclipse, respectively), the working mechanism of this middleware was not the common way Java works. Sherlock depends on external libraries which allow us to communicate with the XBee modules that need to be loaded at the beginning of the execution. Typically, the Java class loader takes the current path as the class path, and loads the libraries which are included at that location. However, UniversAAL uses a different class loader; for efficiency reasons, classes are loaded on demand and dependencies need to be declared beforehand in a manifest file in XML format. This took us several days to figure out how dependencies had to be described in this XML file and where the libraries should be located, especially given the lack of documentation both provided by the organization and existing in the web. This was the most negative point found during the competition, but the technical committee was very helpful in every moment and finally we got to integrate Sherlock into UniversAAL, scoring the highest mark for this criterion.

To sum up, the 1st EvAAL competition was a nice opportunity to test our positioning system in a more realistic environment and check its weakest points in order to know what should be improved. As well, we were able to meet different people working in the same topic, which turned out to be a very enriching experience and a good forum to exchange knowledge and ideas. Regarding the scoring for the proposed system, for each criterion, we summarize the main learnt lessons and future challenges as follows:

- **Accuracy.** Sherlock was designed to provide symbolic locations (e.g. presence of an individual in a building, on certain floor, inside a room, at some part of the room) instead of absolute locations (i.e. coordinates in a three dimensional space). Because of this fact, our system performed well in the detection of the Areas of Interest, but failed in the tracking of a person providing his/her actual absolute location. In order to solve this issue, we are working on the introduction of additional techniques which can be combined with the ones that are already included, so that we can provide three dimensional positioning in a more accurate way. The score for this criterion was 1,8055.
- **Availability.** The chosen algorithm (k-NN using Euclidean Distance as a similarity metric) was efficient enough to score high in this criterion. However, we need to evaluate how the incorporation of new positioning techniques that improve the accuracy of the system may impact the degradation of the availability of the system, since there is a tradeoff between accuracy and efficiency (typically, more accurate estimations may require more computations). The score for this criterion was 9,0193.
- **Complexity of the Installation.** Another weak point of Sherlock, besides the accuracy, was the time it took to install it. We scored 0 points, which turned out to be really bad for the overall score. The current way to deploy the system involves training of the system and it is not very well automatized. Moreover, this was the first time we deployed the positioning system in an unknown environment. In order to solve this, we are researching a way to perform the training of the system in an automatic way in order to reduce the installation time. We also believe that this automatization will eventually lead to increase the accuracy of the system. Besides, an improvement of the tools we used to install the system and perform the training is necessary and complementary to the automatization of the training stage.

- **User Acceptance.** The score for this criterion was 6 points. Currently, the user to be located needs to carry a device (an Arduino board) together with a battery. Since the purpose of this competition is to find positioning systems that can be incorporated in environments where elderly people live, this may be a problem. The elderly can forget to carry the device and, consequently, it is not possible to track them. Since our system is employing mainly wireless radio-frequency based technologies, the user needs to carry some kind of device. However, we are trying to make it as reduced as possible, so that it can be easily carried with no notice. For instance, we are studying the possibility to employ wearable sensors and boards (Arduino Lilypad), which are smaller than the boards we used in the competition and can be incorporated into the clothes or shoes of the person to be located, contributing to the used acceptance of the system.
- **Integrability in AAL Systems.** Undoubtedly, this was the strongest point of our system, scoring 10 points. The component-based design of the system and its encapsulation in a service made it really easy to use. Moreover, we incorporated different standard technologies to access the service, which contributes to software decoupling and reusability of the system. We will keep working hard on this topic to ensure interoperability between our system and others by means of the incorporation of more SOA standards.

5   Related Work

Many research has been done in the field of positioning methods and technologies. Recently, focus is on those techniques which are applicable on indoor environments. Typically, accuracy of these methods is the main goal of those studies.

Some pieces of work only uses a single source of data. That is the case of the Ekahau system [6], which makes use of WiFi tags to make positioning from sub-room level to building level. Similarly, in [1] authors make use of a Bluetooth-based positioning system for location-based advertising. It is based in cell-identification, which presents a high inaccuracy, but it is not relevant for the purpose of the application. Blasco et al. [4] present a positioning system based on ZigBee networks applied to Ambient Assisted Living. It measures the Received Signal Strength and employs a fingerprinting algorithm to compute the user's location.

In order to obtain both indoor and outdoor positioning, Kawaguchi [8] employs WiFi technology. Authors collected information of WiFi access points in a city, tagging them with their GPS approximate location. They did the same on indoor environments, particularly on the city subway. They present a set of LBS which make successful use of such system. Alonso et al. [2] aim to combine WiFi and human motion recognition in order to better estimate the user's location. For that purpose, they use inertial devices like accelerometers or gyroscopes, as well as WiFi devices. They employ fuzzy logic rules in order to compute the locations.

A system combining WiFi and GPS for indoor and outdoor positioning, respectively, can be found in [7]. The purpose of the system is to help people to evacuate a building during an emergency. It employs fingerprinting techniques for indoor positioning, and triangulation outdoors.

In [5], authors present a system based on sensor fusion. They try to combine different sources of input data which are useful for positioning purposes. This, together with map knowledge, leads to an improvement of the accuracy of the system, since it employs a probabilistic method which has physical limitations into account, as well as the robustness – failure of some sensors is not critical because there is a wide variety of them available.

6   Conclusions and Future Work

In this paper, we have presented the design of a reusable positioning service by means of a service-based architecture, based on interoperable components which can be substituted in runtime to guarantee the fulfillment of certain non-functional requirements. This can serve as a starting point to design services in an ubiquitous computing environment in a similar way. In a near future, we will work on the formalization of this design process for ubiquitous computing services.

We have shown how different combinations of technologies and positioning methods are possible thanks to the careful design of common abstract interfaces that have to be implemented by different components. The use of such interfaces makes all the parts in the system agnostic from each other, loosening the coupling between them and making the system adaptable and customizable. The positioning service gives support to the development of context-aware systems, but it is itself context-aware and adapts to the external conditions and needs.

The hybrid approach opens a lot of possibilities to LBS designers: their applications can obtain both indoor and outdoor positioning; they are not limited to a single technology or positioning method, nor constrained by a certain architecture. The reusability of the system is much more enhanced thanks to these design decisions. Moreover, this facilitates the reconfiguration based on different combinations of technologies and positioning techniques, only by adding and removing the corresponding components, without needing to design or implement a whole positioning system.

The EvAAL competition was a very positive experience to test Sherlock in a real, a priori unknown, environment with strong constraints, specially regarding time. It helped us to discover the main disadvantages, as well as the strengths, of our system, so we know what are the next steps to perform in order to improve the system are. Besides, the competition was a good opportunity to make contact with other experts in this field, which turned out to be a very enriching experience and a good place to share knowledge. This design can help to alleviate the major problems present in the field of positioning systems. However, there are other challenges which have to be taken into account in the design of this system, and which we will work in the future:

- Positioning is based in the assumption of fixed base stations. Moreover, indoor positioning often requires training of the system, or adjustment of a radio propagation model. However, there are scenarios where this previous stage is not possible, or even useless because the environment has changed and the infrastructure might be destroyed. Such is the case of a catastrophe, like a fire in a building where the existing infrastructure may be burning. Thus, the positioning system should be able to obtain positioning of some entities given that the base stations are also mobile, but its position is known by other means.

– Another challenge concerns the low resources some mobile devices have. Performing measurements of signals, reporting them or computing its own location can be very costly. In these cases, positioning could be done in a cooperative way: if the mobile device detects other devices which are near, it can request their position and take it as its own.

– The architectures we have seen often require a centralized server, becomes a bottleneck and a single point of failure. Although we can distribute, replicate and balance the load of the server to ease these problems, there can be cases were such a server is not present. Then, we would need to address a Mobile Ad-Hoc Network (MANET) in such a way where the most powerful devices should compute their own locations, but also respond to requests of other devices with low resources. This network should count on a middleware which deliver requests uniformly among the devices, saving messages and ensuring the quality of the service.

References

1. Aalto, L., Gothlin, N., Korhonen, J., Ojala, T.: Bluetooth and WAP Push Based Location-Aware Mobile Advertising System. In: MobiSys 2004 (2004)
2. Alonso, J.M., Álvarez, A., Trivino, G., Hernández, N., Herranz, F., Ocaña, M.:: Towards People Indoor Localization Combining WiFi and Human Motion Recognition. XV Congreso Español sobre Tecnologías y Lógica Fuzzy (2010)
3. Arduino, http://www.arduino.cc
4. Blasco, R., Marco, Á., Casas, R., Ibarz, A., Coarasa, V., Asensio, Á.: Indoor Localization Based on Neural Networks for Non-dedicated ZigBee Networks in AAL. In: Cabestany, J., Sandoval, F., Prieto, A., Corchado, J.M. (eds.) IWANN 2009, Part I. LNCS, vol. 5517, pp. 1113–1120. Springer, Heidelberg (2009)
5. Bohn, J., Vogt, H.: Robust Probabilistic Positioning based on High-Level Sensor-Fusion and Map Knowledge. Technical Report No. 421
6. Ekahau, http://www.ekahau.com/
7. Herranz, F., Ocaña, M., Bergasa, L.M., Sotelo, M.A., Barea, R., López, E., Hernández, N.: Sistema de Localización GPS y WiFi sobre PDA aplicado a un Sistema de Evacuación de Emergencia
8. Kawaguchi, N.: WiFi Location Information System for Both Indoors and Outdoors. In: Omatu, S., Rocha, M.P., Bravo, J., Fernández, F., Corchado, E., Bustillo, A., Corchado, J.M. (eds.) IWANN 2009, Part I. LNCS, vol. 5518, pp. 638–645. Springer, Heidelberg (2009)
9. Kjærgaard, M.B.: A Taxonomy for Radio Location Fingerprinting. In: Hightower, J., Schiele, B., Strang, T. (eds.) LoCA 2007. LNCS, vol. 4718, pp. 139–156. Springer, Heidelberg (2007)

10. Lin, T.N., Lin, P.C.: Performance Comparison of Indoor Positioning Techniques based on Location Fingerprinting in Wireless Networks (2005)
11. Liu, H., Darabi, H., Banerjee, P., Liu, J.: Survey of Wireless Indoor Positioning Techniques and Systems. IEEE Transactions on Systems, Man and Cybernetics Part C: Applications and Reviews 37(6) (2007)
12. Pahlavan, K., Li, X., Makela, J.P.: Indoor geolocation science and technology. IEEE Communications Magazine, 112–118 (2002)
13. Rodríguez-Domínguez, C., Benghazi, K., Noguera, M., Bermúdez-Edo, M., Garrido, J.L.: Dynamic Ontology-Based Redefinition of Events Intended to Support the Communication of Complex Information in Ubiquitous Computing. Journal of Network Protocols and Algorithms 2(3) ISSN 1943-3581
14. Ruiz-López, T., Garrido, J.L., Benghazi, K., Chung, L.: A Survey on Indoor Positioning Systems: Foreseeing a Quality Design. In: de Leon F. de Carvalho, A.P., Rodríguez-González, S., De Paz Santana, J.F., Rodríguez, J.M.C. (eds.) Distributed Computing and Artificial Intelligence. AISC, vol. 79, pp. 373–380. Springer, Heidelberg (2010)

Precision Indoor Objects Positioning
Based on Phase Measurements of Microwave Signals

Igor Shirokov

Department of Radio Engineering, Sevastopol National Technical University,
Universitetskaya 33, Sevastopol, Ukraine, 99053
shirokov@ieee.org

Abstract. Object positioning based on phase method measures the distances among transponders (placed on objects) and beacons (placed at reference points) in terms of microwave phase difference or in parts of wavelengths. Such approach assumes a high resolution in distance determination. Specifically, the homodyne method considers microwave phase difference measurements. The beacons are placed in a room and radiate the microwave signals. The transponders are devices wearable by elders/disabled who have to be located. The transponders shift the frequencies of microwave signals (each transponder its own frequency shift) and reradiate the frequency-transformed microwave signals back in the directions of beacons. Each beacon selects the low-frequency difference signals and measures the phase differences between these signals and the reference one. Based on these measurements the distances to transponders are calculated.

Keywords: Microwave antennas, Microwave phase measurements, Homodyne method of frequency transformation, Transponder, Microwave phase shifter, Microwave mixer.

1   Introduction

Although microwave propagation offers a good opportunity for object positioning, the use of the pulse radar method for measuring distances and angles are quite unsuitable for indoor applications. The resolution of this method is too low and there is a minimal distance requirement of the pulse radar measurement that is usually higher than the room size.

On the other hand, the resolution of the phase method of distance measurements is determined by the microwave length. Depending on the wavelength one can reach an accuracy of 10 mm and better [1].

In this paper we present a new method for positioning of people in indoors environment. Positioning is calculated in terms of distances measurements, from the beacons to transponders that are wearable by elders/disabled. The microwave phase progression measurements are used for these purposes. No doubts, the phase method causes an ambiguity because the phase measurements can only have values in an interval between 0-2π. In this paper the way of bypassing this problem is also discussed.

S. Chessa and S. Knauth (Eds.): EvAAL 2011, CCIS 309, pp. 80–91, 2012.

Furthermore, the task of simultaneous positioning of several objects is also important, especially in applications that need to track several people concurrently. In these cases, the number of tracked people may scale up especially in applications deployed in hospitals or offices, and in these cases the problem of objects differentiating appears.

Furthermore, the electromagnetic compatibility (EMC) of functioning of several radio engineering units must be taken into account. The simultaneous functioning of these units has not to deteriorate the differentiating of the object and its positioning. The way of solving this problem is discussed in the paper.

Further, the people's tracking assumes radiating of electromagnetic waves. Certainly, this radiation should not affect the human health. The system radiating power must be as small as possible in this case. The radiating of electromagnetic energy from the people's wearable devices has to be excluded, if possible. This issue is discussed in the paper as well.

Besides the above mentioned technical and healthcare aspects, localization and tracking systems have also to be economic, and, to this aim, all of system components must have a simple design, the hardware deployment should reduce the required manpower, and the system power consumption must be as small as possible. In other words the system must satisfy the demands of state-of-art tendencies of so called "green communication". These aspects are also discussed in the paper.

2   Approach to a Problem

The system implementation, which is free from mentioned problems, assumes using of homodyne method of microwave phase measurements, which is well developed in author's previous works [2]–[6]. The further developing of this approach takes place in the paper.

Realizing the homodyne method of microwave phase measurements and, consequently, distances determination within a room, we offer to place the radio beacons B1 and B2 along the extended wall and at the certain distance b each from another, as it is shown in Fig.1.

The positioning of objects is characterized by the distances d_{ij} from the objects to each beacon, as it is shown in Fig.1.

The distance among beacons is an important system parameter. The number of beacons can be higher than 2 and they can be placed along the different room walls. The positioning of the beacons ensures the elimination of doubts in distance determination and it ensures the coverage of the entire environment, at arbitrary distances from beacon(s) to object(s). However these aspects are out of the scope of the paper, and doubts elimination is solved organizationally.

For this reason we assume that the system operates in a room only. Usually the material of the wall is not transparent for microwaves (we do not consider wooden walls) at all, or signals are damped very much. In this case additional beacons must be installed in the neighboring rooms, in this way the system can track the person also when he/she moves to other rooms.

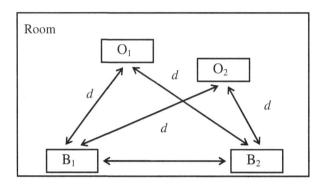

Fig. 1. Placing the beacons and the objects in the room

The transponders are worn by people O1 and O2 that have to be located. The number of objects can be arbitrary, but with certain restrictions, which will be discussed later. In the paper we will discuss the simultaneous operating of two transponders, not changing the approach to the general problem.

Taking into account the system base b and all of distances d_{ij}, we can determine the objects positions in Cartesian coordinate system with respect to system base and beacons easily enough.

Certainly, the object positioning will be carried out in a plane. The heights of beacon antennas and transponder antennas placement must be similar. Violating this rule results in large errors in the distances measurements.

However, this problem can be solved easily by the placing of additional (third) beacon on a plane of the wall on the certain distance from system base b. The heights of beacons placing and transponders placing can be arbitrary in this case; the calculating routine will solve this problem.

The block diagrams of each transponder and each beacon are shown in Fig. 2.

Each transponder, which is placed on the object, consists of microwave antenna, controlled transmission phase shifter (CTPS), one-port microwave transistor amplifier (OPTA), and low-frequency oscillator of transponder (LFOT).

Each beacon consists of microwave oscillator (MWO), microwave directional coupler (MDC) microwave transmitting antenna, microwave receiving antenna, microwave mixer (MMIX), low-frequency mixer (LMIX), low-frequency heterodyne (LHET), selective amplifier-limiter (SALIM), low-frequency oscillator of beacon (LFOB), and phase detector (PD).

The line "Microwave Frequencies" assumes controlling of microwave oscillator frequencies. The frequency changing is of need for adequate distance determination. The frequencies of different beacons must be different but closely spaced. The problem of frequency choosing will be discussed later.

The phase differences of low-frequency signals are obtained on the line "Phase Differences".

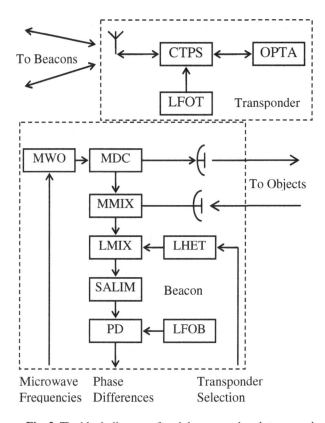

Fig. 2. The block diagram of each beacon and each transponder

These phase differences of low-frequency signals contain the information representing the phase progression of microwave signals.

The line "Transponder Selection" assumes frequency controlling of low-frequency heterodyne. This Figure represents the serial treating of transponder signals. Obviously, the use of parallel chains after the microwave mixer assumes parallel signal treating. The processing time will be lower, but the hardware cost will be higher in this case.

3   Base Equations

Each ith beacon radiates the microwave signal that can be described as

$$u_{i1}(t) = U_{i0} \sin\left[\omega_{i0}t + \varphi_{i0}\right],$$

where U_{i0} is the amplitude, ω_{i0} is the frequency, and φ_{i0} is the initial phase.

These oscillations are radiated in the direction of inner part of the room where the jth object is placed. The microwave, propagated along the distance d_{ij}, obtains the attenuation A_{ij} and phase progression $k_{i0}d_{ij}$:

$$u_{ij2}(t) = A_{ij}U_{i0}\sin\left[\omega_{i0}t + k_{i0}d_{ij} + \varphi_{i0}\right],$$

where $k_{i0} = 2\pi/\lambda_{i0}$ is the propagation constant, λ_{i0} is the wavelength.

The jth transponder receives this microwave signal with its microwave antenna. Then the controlled transmission phase shifter implements the monotonous change of microwave-signal phase over the period T_j of the low-frequency oscillations on the value π. The low-frequency oscillator generates these oscillations with certain frequency stability. The value of this stability will be discussed later.

The shown block diagram assumes passing of microwave signal thru the phase shifter twice. So, the microwave-signal phase will be changed on the value 2π over the period T_j of the low-frequency oscillations, as it is shown in Fig. 3a or in Fig.3b. The change of microwave-signal phase over the period T_j of the low-frequency oscillations on the value 2π is tantamount to the frequency shift [7] of microwave signal on the frequency $\Omega_j = 2\pi/T_j$. In a certain assumption, this technical solution is equivalent to Doppler's frequency shifting.

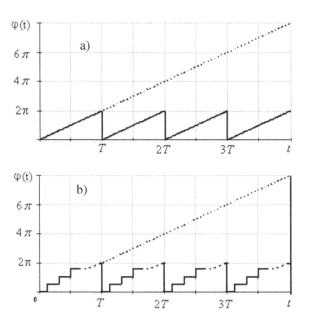

Fig. 3. The law of microwave signal phase changing

The amount of frequency shift is chosen small. Really, F_j ($F_j = \Omega_j / 2\pi$) is equal to tens of kilohertzes or closely and at any case it does not exceed the value in hundred kilohertzes.

One more feature is observed in this case: the initial phase of the controlling low-frequency oscillations φ_{jL} is transferred into the microwave-signal phase directly, without any changes. This feature was put on a basis of all author's previous investigations [2]–[6].

After the controlled phase shifter the microwave signal is amplified by the one-port microwave transistor amplifier [8]. This microwave amplifier possesses the highest simplicity of design implementation, has very low power consumption, and has excellent noise characteristics. Described amplifier operates in narrow frequency band, but this feature is not dramatic one in our case. Furthermore, the perfect antenna matching can be implemented in a narrow frequency band as well. Thus, we obtain the microwave signal amplifying in 20-30 dB with the noise factor $N_F = 0.3$ dB at 1.5 GHz.

Further, the amplified microwave signal passes thru the phase shifter again and obtains the frequency and phase shift. The frequency/phase transformed microwave signal will be

$$u_{ij3}(t) = A'_{ij} \, U_{i0} \sin\left[\left(\omega_{i0} + \Omega_j\right)t + k_{i0}d_{ij} + \varphi_{i0} + \varphi_{jL}\right],$$

where A'_{ij} takes into account the transponder gain.

The transponder gain determines the operating distance of the system only and it does not affect the accuracy of object positioning. So, we will assume the gain of transponder is equal to 1 ($A'_{ij} = A_{ij}$). Transponder reradiates this frequency/phase transformed microwave signal back in the beacon direction. In the beacon the secondary received microwave signal will be

$$u_{ij4}(t) = A_{ij}^2 U_{i0} \sin\left[\left(\omega_{i0} + \Omega_j\right)t + k_{i0}d_i + k'_{i0}d_{ij} + \varphi_{i0} + \varphi_{jL}\right],$$

where k'_{i0} takes into account the frequency shift $\omega_{i0} + \Omega_j$.

The frequency shift Ω_j is much lower than the initial frequency ω_{i0} (e.g. $f_{i0} = \omega_{i0}/2\pi = 1.5$ GHz and $F = (10...100)$ kHz), then $k'_{i0} \approx k_{i0}$. This secondary received signal is mixed with the original microwave signal and at the mixer output the low-frequency signal of difference is selected. This low-frequency signal will be

$$u_{ij5}(t) = A_{ij}^2 U_{i0} \sin\left[\Omega_j t + 2k_{i0}d_{ij} + \varphi_{jL}\right]. \qquad (1)$$

As we can see from (1), the initial frequency ω_{i0} and the initial phase φ_{i0} of origin microwave signal both are subtracted in the mixer. The only double phase progression $2k_{i0}d_{ij}$ of the microwave signal is of interest for the distance definition.

The low-frequency signals from each jth transponder are obtained at the output of each mixer of each ith beacon [9] and [10], but the phase shift will be unique for each pair beacon-transponder and it will be determined by each distance d_{ij}. As the frequencies of signals Ω_j from different transponders are quite different, it is inconvenient to measure the phase differences between these signals and the reference one. Avoiding this problem the heterodyning of received signal is proposed. The frequency of heterodyne Ω_i in i^{th} beacon is chosen so that the difference $\Omega_i - \Omega_j$ remains constant and the one is equal to 10 kHz, for example. The signal with such frequency is amplified up to limitation and it will be described as

$$u_{ij6}(t) = U_0 \sin\left[\Omega_{ij}t + 2k_{i0}d_{ij} + \varphi_{jL} - \varphi_{iH}\right],$$

where $\Omega_{ij} = \Omega_i - \Omega_j$, φ_{iH} is the initial phase of heterodyne signal. The phase of this signals is compared with the phase of low-frequency reference signal with the same frequency $\Omega = \Omega_{ij}$. So, the phase detector output data Ψ_{ij} will be proportional to value

$$\Psi_{ij} \sim 2k_{i0}d_{ij} + \Delta\Omega t + \varphi,$$

where $\Delta\Omega$ is the reduced mutual frequency instability of all of low-frequency oscillators, φ is the sum of all of initial phases of all of low-frequency oscillators.

Thus, analyzing the data Ψ_{ij}, we can determine each of distances d_{ij}.

4   Errors and Processing Algorithm

The term $\Delta\Omega t$ is the dynamic error of phase measurements, φ is the static one. However, what value of the error we are talking about? For signal frequency in 10 kHz the absolute frequency instability of crystal oscillator does not exceed 0.1 Hz. For the signal processing time in 10 ms the dynamic error will be 0.36°, that corresponds to distance determination error in 0.2 mm (twice value) for the frequency of microwave signal in 1.5 GHz. Certainly, we can neglect the dynamic error $\Delta\Omega t$.

The static error φ is constant for all time of measuring process (ever since all of oscillators are started up). We can exclude this error by the calibration procedure, but it will be excluded automatically in a result of processing-algorithm implementation.

Thus, the only thing we must ensure is the high frequency stability of each low-frequency oscillator. In other words, the phase mismatch between any two oscillators can not exceed the phase measurements resolution during the whole time of measuring procedure implementation. If the algorithm of coordinates' determination is not time-consuming, and the number of iterations is not high, the use of ordinary crystal oscillators will be the best solution for technical implementation.

A little bit different approach we must use to the determination of microwave-oscillator frequency instability. Here the measured distance plays an important role. Let assume the maximal operating distance d_{ij} in 50 m and maximal error in distance determination Δd_{ij} in 1 mm (the phase measurements error in 1.2°), then for frequency in 1.5 GHz the maximal frequency instability $\Delta f_0 / f_0$ will be 3 ppm. Such value of frequency instability is realized by temperature stabilizing of reference crystal oscillator.

Generally, it is possible to measure a phase difference between 0 and 2π. The phase progression $k_{i0} d_{ij}$ will be represented as $2\pi n + k_{i0} \Delta d$, where n is integer. In order to avoid this problem we serially change the operating frequency of microwave oscillator of each beacon [11], [12] and we measure the phase differences between the reference low-frequency oscillator signal and low-frequency mixer output signal. At first time we fix this phase difference as $\Delta \varphi_1$ and fix the frequency f_1. After that we change the frequency of microwave oscillator till the phase difference will be $\Delta \varphi_2 = \Delta \varphi_1 + 2\pi = \Delta \varphi_1$, then we fix the frequency f_2 and calculate the distance as

$$d_{ij} = \frac{c}{2(f_1 - f_2)}.$$

Certainly, these calculations yield the rough results of distance determination. These calculations let us obtain the number of phase cycles n and the possibility to determine the distance in terms of integer numbers of wavelengths. The exact value of distance d_{ij} can be obtained by measuring the phase difference $k_{i0} \Delta d_{ij}$. Taking into consideration the accuracy of phase measurements in 1.4° (8 digits) and possible wavelength in 0.2 m, the resolution in distance determination will be about 1 mm. We should understand that the measured distance will be conditional distance, taking into account antennas phase centers and all feeder lengths.

Further, as each beacon operates as stand alone unit, there is a possibility to measure the phase difference between beacons mixers output signals. Mentioned opportunity let us improve the accuracy of coordinate determination, as it was pointed out in [13], [14].

In case of measurements of phase difference between two low frequency signals from two beacons, the frequency stability of transponder low frequency oscillator is not critical matter.

5   Equipment Implementation

Transponder has the simplest design and the lowest power consumption. Besides power supply chains and microcontroller, transponder contains three microwave parts: the microwave antenna, the controlled transmission phase shifter of four/five-digits (16/32 steps), and one-port microwave transistor amplifier. The power consumption of these units not exceeds few milliWatts. The nanoWatt RISC microcontroller with crystal oscillator represents the low-frequency oscillator.

Microcontroller outputs drive the control inputs of phase shifter directly. The frequency of crystal resonator represents the ID of transponder. This is the simplest technical solution, but it will be useful for presentation purpose only. We can implement several standard frequencies for crystal resonator. In our case these frequencies will be 16,000 MHz and 16,384 MHz. So, we will obtain two ID frequencies in 32 kHz and 31.25 kHz. A little bit complication of transponder design will result in obtaining of large number of ID frequencies in a range from 10 kHz up to 100 kHz with the step in 0.5 kHz. The value of frequency step is determined by the pass-band of low-frequency processing chains of the beacon. Further narrowing of pass-band is undesirable, the processing time will increase in this case.

As a unit for presentation transponder has size 120×120×20 mm^3. The real size of PCB is much less. These dimensions depend on the wavelength, and the top side of transponder is the shield. In the center of top side there is placed whip antenna. The real value of operating frequency is 1300 MHz.

The appearance of transponder is shown in fig. 4.

Fig. 4. Transponder design

The design of transponder can be different. It can be wearable unit with arbitrary oriented antenna. The antenna design in this case and the influence of human body on microwave signal amplitude and phase is separate scientific issue.

The power consumption of transponder is about 50 mW. Power supplying is two cells of A-size.

The cost of the beacon is higher, but the design remains be simple, see fig. 5.

In a beacon we use two patch antennas on a single board rather than Y-circulator and single antenna. Patches are separated on a certain distance. This technical solution ensures the better decoupling of transmitting and receiving paths. We obtained the decoupling in 40 dB. None Y-circulator ensures such value. In this case the phase center of equivalent antenna will be in the middle point (between the patches).

The size of the beacon is 120×180×30 mm^3. The large dimensions determine the board of antennas (two patches on a single board). Now processing chains are placed on a separate board for evaluation purposes only. This board is attached to antennas board directly. Two short microwave feeders are used for these boards connection.

Fig. 5. Beacon design

The processing unit consists of simple microwave chains (see fig.2), low-frequency chains, and microcontroller with built-in CAN-module. Microcontroller commands the frequencies of microwave oscillator and low-frequency heterodyne. By means of built-in capture module it measures the phase difference between low-frequency SALIM output signal and interruption signal of own oscillator.

Then the raw data are transferred via CAN-interface to the adapter module.

The beacon will be on a support, or it can be mounted on a room wall directly. Patch ensures the radiating in single hemisphere.

The number of beacons on a single CAN-line can reach huge value. The transmission speed of CAN-interface was chosen in 64 kbit/s. That ensures the length of CAN-line in 1 km. In a test version of equipment we implement two beacons only.

The adapter module collects the raw data from beacons via CAN-interface and transmits these data to PC via Ethernet. The simplest UDP protocol is used. This module ensures the power supplying of beacons too. So, the 4-core cable is used for connection of all units (two cores for power supplying and two cores for CAN-line). The power consumption of each beacon not exceeds 300 mW.

The size of adapter module is 80×110 mm^2 (PCB) and 30 mm of high.

The design of adapter module is shown in fig. 6.

PC calculates the distances between the beacons and transponders and plots the transponder moving. The data refresh time is about 1 s. It depends on phase measurements iterations in the beacon and it is not limited by interfaces and PC productivity. We can reduce the measurements and the calculations accordingly to a minimum by using of tracking mode.

Fig. 6. Adapter module design

6   Restrictions

Complex indoor environments may produce multipath microwave propagation. First patch of the beacon emits microwave signal within entire room space and the scattered microwave signals are received with another patch of the beacon. But these scattered signals do not interfere with the useful signal because the last has the frequency shift. Only received by the transponder the scattered signal obtains the same frequency shift, but this signal has much lower amplitude than direct one. Surely, the presence of bulk metal in a room will disturb the normal system operation, as well as operation of any other radio engineering system.

The number of transponders operating simultaneously in a room is large and it was discussed above. But certain restriction appears due to the signals mixing. The combinatorial components can interfere with useful signal. The careful ID frequency choosing will eliminate this problem. In any case, this problem will be actual for large number of persons in a room, this is a rare event.

7   Conclusion

We presented equipment for indoor precision object positioning. The considered equipment has a simple design and the low cost, while keeping a high precision, and the equipment installation does not demand the extended manpower. The paper also presents the routines for computing the location of people.

The transponder, which is wearable by elders/disabled, does not generate any radio signals. It only receives and retransmits the microwave signal from beacon(s). So, the intensity of electromagnetic field in man's nearby environment is very low, that does not affect on human health.

The theoretical investigations concerning the system accuracy give good results, which are confirmed by author's previous experimental investigations in this field [5]. The final conclusions will be made after the real equipment testing.

The system is at the stage of a proposal. Some of system modules are now being improved. As the system assumes the radar approach the energy of the system is very weak. So, the accurate adjusting of transmitter, transponder, and receiver has to be implemented. The main goal of this adjusting is the ensuring of declared system operation range. The increasing of transmitter out power is the worst way of this problem solving. The system must ensure so called "green communication." Now the output microwave power of transmitter does not exceed 15 dBm.

References

1. Pestrjakov, V.B.: Phase radio engineering systems, Moscow, Soviet Radio, 468 p. (1968) (in Russian)
2. Shirokov, I.B., Bondjuk, V.V.: Distance measurement by a phase method. In: Proc. SVMI Named P.S. Nakhimov of Naval Forces of Ukraine, Sevastopol, vol. 1(4), pp. 152–155 (2004) (in Russian)
3. Shirokov, I.B., Shaban, S.: Method of Measurement of Fluctuations of Phase progression and Angle-of-Arrival of Microwave, Pat. Ukraine, # 58814A, pub. In: B. # 8, August 15, G01R29/08, 6 p. (2003) (in Ukrainian)
4. Shirokov, I.B., Gimpilevich, Y.B.: Generalized mathematical model of homodyne frequency conversion method under a periodic variation in sounding signal phase shift. Telecommunications and Radio Engineering (English Translation of Elektrosvyaz and Radiotekhnika) 66(12), 1057–1065 (2007)
5. Shirokov, I.B., Gimpilevich, Y.B.: Experimental Investigation of Amplitude and Phase Progression Fluctuation on Microwave Line-of-Sight Link. In: IEEE AP-S & CNC/USNC/URSI Symposium, Toronto, Ontario, Canada, July 11-17, pp. 1–4 (2010)
6. Shirokov, I.B.: Near-field amplitude and phase measurements in antenna aperture plane. In: The 5th ESA Int. Workshop on Tracking, Telemetry and Command Systems for Ground and Space Applications, European Space Technology Centre (ESTEC) in Noordwijk, The Netherlands, September 21-23, 5 p. (2010)
7. Jaffe, J.S., Mackey, R.C.: Microwave Frequency Translator. IEEE Trans. on Microwave Theory and Techniques 13, 371–378 (1965)
8. Venguer, A.P., Medina, J.L., Chávez, R.A., Velázquez, A.: Low Noise One-Port Microwave Transistor Amplifier. Microwave and Optical Technology Letters 33(2), 100–104 (2002)
9. Shirokov, I.B.: The Method of Radio Frequency Identification, Pat. Ukraine, #91937, Pub. in Bull. #17, September 10, MPC G01R 29/08, 6 p. (2010) (in Ukrainian)
10. Shirokov, I.B.: The Multitag Microwave RFID System. IEEE Trans. on Microwave Theory and Techniques 57(5, Pt. 2), 1362–1369 (2009)
11. Shirokov, I.B.: The Method of Distance Measurement from Measuring Station to Transponder, Pat. Ukraine, #93645 pub. in Bull. #4, February 25, MPC G01S 13/32, 7 p. (2011) (in Ukrainian)
12. Shirokov, I.B.: The Method of Distance Measurement, Pat. of Ukraine, #94529 pub. in Bull. #9, May 10, MPC G01S 13/32, 7 p. (2011) (in Ukrainian)
13. Shirokov, I.B.: The Positioning of Space Objects Based on Microwave Angle-of-Arrival Measurements. In: The 4th ESA Int. Workshop on Tracking, Telemetry and Command Systems for Space Applications, Darmstadt, Germany, September 11-14, 7 p. (2007)
14. Shirokov, I.B., Ponyatenko, A., Kulish, O.: The Measurement of Angle-of-arrival of Microwave in a Task of Precision Landing of Aircraft. In: Progress In Electromagnetics Research Symposium, PIERS 2008, Cambridge, MA, USA, July 2-6, pp. 153–159 (2008)

The n-Core Polaris Real-Time Locating System at the EvAAL Competition

Dante I. Tapia[1,2], Óscar García[1,2], Ricardo S. Alonso[1,2], Fabio Guevara[1],
Jorge Catalina[1], Raúl A. Bravo[2], and Juan M. Corchado[2]

[1] R&D Department, Nebusens, S.L., Scientific Park of the University of Salamanca,
Edificio M2, Calle Adaja, s/n, 37185, Villamayor de la Armuña, Salamanca, Spain
[2] Department of Computer Science and Automation, University of Salamanca,
Plaza de la Merced, s/n, 37008, Salamanca, Spain
{dante.tapia,oscar.garcia,ricardo.alonso,
fabio.guevara,jorge.catalina}@nebusens.com,
{dantetapia,oscgar,ralorin,raulabel,corchado}@usal.es

Abstract. One of the most important technologies used to provide context-awareness in Ambient Assisted Living environments is Wireless Sensor Networks (WSNs). Wireless Sensor Networks comprise an ideal technology to develop Real-Time Locating Systems (RTLS) aimed at indoor environments, where existing global navigation satellite systems do not work correctly. In this sense, Nebusens[1] and the BISITE Research Group[2] of the University of Salamanca have developed n-Core Polaris, a new indoor and outdoor RTLS based on ZigBee WSNs and an innovative set of locating and automation engines. n-Core Polaris is based on the n-Core platform, a hardware and software platform intended for developing and deploying easily and quickly a wide variety of WSN applications based on the ZigBee standard. This paper describes the n-Core Polaris system, as well as the experiments made during the first EvAAL Competition on Indoor Localization and Tracking, whose results demonstrate the effectiveness of n-Core Polaris in indoor environments.

Keywords: Ambient Assisted Living, Real-Time Locating Systems, Wireless Sensor Networks, ZigBee, Web Services.

1   Introduction

People are currently surrounded by technology which tries to increase their quality of life and facilitate their daily activities. However, there are situations where technology is difficult to handle or people have a lack of knowledge to use it. Ambient Assisted Living (AAL) tries to adapt the technology to the people's needs by means of omnipresent computing elements which communicate among them in a ubiquitous way [1]. In addition, the continuous advancement in mobile computing makes it possible to obtain information about the context and also to react physically to it in

---

[1] http://www.nebusens.com
[2] http://bisite.usal.es

S. Chessa and S. Knauth (Eds.): EvAAL 2011, CCIS 309, pp. 92–106, 2012.
© Springer-Verlag Berlin Heidelberg 2012

more innovative ways. In this sense, it is necessary to develop new infrastructures capable of providing adaptable and compatible frameworks, allowing access to functionalities regardless of time and location restrictions.

Wireless Sensor Networks (WSN) are used for gathering the information needed by AAL environments, whether in home automation, industrial applications or smart hospitals. One of the most interesting applications for WSNs is Real-Time Locating Systems (RTLS). The most important factors in the locating process are the kinds of sensors used and the techniques applied for the calculation of the position based on the information recovered by these sensors. Although outdoor locating is well covered by systems such as the current GPS (Global Positioning System) or the future Galileo, indoor locating needs still more development, especially with respect to accuracy and low-cost and efficient infrastructures [2]. Therefore, it is necessary to develop Real-Time Locating Systems that allow performing efficient indoor locating in terms of precision and optimization of resources. This optimization of resources includes the reduction of the costs and size of the sensor infrastructure involved on the locating system. In this regard, the use of optimized locating techniques allows obtaining more accurate locations using even fewer sensors and with less computational requirements [2].

There are several wireless technologies used by indoor RTLS, such as RFID (Radio Frequency IDentification) [3], Wi-Fi [4], UWB (Ultra Wide Band) [5] and ZigBee [6]. However, independently of the technology used, it is necessary to establish mathematical models that allow determining the position of a person or object based on the signals recovered by the sensors infrastructure. The position can be calculated by means of several locating techniques, such as *signpost*, *fingerprinting*, *triangulation*, *trilateration* and *multilateration* [6]. However, all of them must deal with important problems when trying to develop a precise locating system that uses WSNs in its infrastructure, especially for indoor environments.

In this regard, this paper presents n-Core Polaris [7], an innovative Real-Time Locating System that features an outstanding precision, flexibility and automation integration. n-Core Polaris is based on n-Core [8], a hardware and software platform intended for developing and deploying easily and quickly a wide variety of WSN applications based on the ZigBee standard. n-Core Polaris exploits the unlimited potential of the n-Core platform, taking advantage of the advanced set of features of the n-Core Sirius devices and the n-Core Application Programming Interface. The main features of n-Core Polaris include extremely easy set-up and deployment; intuitive mobile and desktop interfaces; simple definition of restricted areas according to the users' permissions; and full integration with a wide range of sensors and actuators.

In order to demonstrate the effectiveness of n-Core Polaris in indoor environments, Nebusens and the BISITE Research Group participated in the first International Competition on Indoor Localization and Tracking (EvAAL 2011) [9], organized by the Ambient-Assisted Living Open Association (AALOA) [10], which took place in the Experimental Research Center in Applications and Services for Ambient Intelligence (CIAMI) [11] in Valencia (Spain) on July 2011, and whose results were announced in the AAL Forum in Lecce (Italy) at the end of September 2011.

This paper is structured as follows. The next section explains the problem description, as well as a comparison among the most widely used wireless technologies to build indoor RTLSs. Then, Section 3 depicts the main characteristics of the n-Core Polaris RTLS. After that, Section 4 describes the experiments carried out in a real scenario during the EvAAL 2011 competition to test the performance of different indoor RTLSs, as well as the results obtained by n-Core Polaris. Finally, Section 5 presents the conclusions obtained so far.

2   Problem Description

The emergence of Ambient Assisted Living involves substantial changes in the design of systems, since it is necessary to provide features which enable a ubiquitous computing and communication and also an intelligent interaction with users. The aim of AAL is to look for an omnipresent computing by means of services and applications that use computing elements which can watch and communicate one another [1]. Ambient Assisted Living proposes new ways of interaction between people and technology, making the latter to be adapted to the people's necessities and the environment where they are. This kind of interaction is achieved by means of technology that is embedded, non-invasive and transparent for users. In this regard, users' locations given by Real-Time Locating Systems represent key context information to adapt systems to people's needs and preferences.

Real-Time Locating Systems can be categorized by the kind of its wireless sensor infrastructure and by the locating techniques used to calculate the position of the tags. This way, there is a combination of several wireless technologies, such as RFID, Wi-Fi, UWB and ZigBee, and also a wide range of locating techniques that can be used to determine the position of the tags. Among the most widely used locating techniques we have *signpost*, *fingerprinting*, *triangulation*, *trilateration* and *multilateration* [6] [12]. The set of the locating techniques that an RTLS integrates is known as the *locating engine* [6].

A widespread technology used in Real-Time Locating Systems is *Radio Frequency IDentification* (RFID) [3]. In this case, the RFID readers act as *exciters* transmitting continuously a radio frequency signal that is collected by the RFID tags, which in turn respond to the readers by sending their identification numbers. In these kinds of locating systems, each reader covers a certain zone through its radio frequency signal, known as *reading field*. When a tag passes through the reading field of the reader, it is said that the tag *is* in that zone.

Locating systems based on *Wireless Fidelity* (Wi-Fi) take advantage of Wi-Fi WLANs (Wireless Local Area Networks) working in the 2.4GHz and 5.8GHz ISM (Industrial, Scientific and Medical) bands to calculate the positions of the mobile devices (i.e., tags) [4]. A wide range of locating techniques, then, can be used for processing the Wi-Fi signals and determining the position of the tags, including signpost, fingerprinting or trilateration. However, locating systems based on Wi-Fi present some problems such as the interferences with existing data transmissions and the high power consumption by the Wi-Fi tags.

Ultra-Wide Band (UWB) is a technology which has been recently introduced to develop these kinds of systems. As it works at high frequencies (the band covers from 3.1GHz to 10.6 GHz in the USA) [5], it allows to achieve very accurate location estimations. However, at such frequencies the electromagnetic waves suffer a great attenuation by objects (e.g., walls) so its use on indoor RTLS systems presents important problems, especially the ground reflection effect due the high frequencies used.

ZigBee is another interesting technology to build RTLS. The ZigBee standard is specially intended to implement Wireless Sensor Networks and, as Wi-Fi and Bluetooth, can work in the 2.4GHz ISM band, but also can work on the 868–915MHz band. Different locating techniques based on RSSI and LQI can be used on ZigBee WSNs (e.g., signpost or trilateration). Moreover, it allows building networks or more than 65,000 nodes in star, cluster-tree and mesh topologies [6]. ZigBee is, indeed, the wireless technology selected for our research.

Table 1 shows a comparison between the main wireless technologies when implementing Real-Time Locating Systems. In this table, it can be seen a summary of the main advantages and drawbacks of RTLSs based on each technology.

Table 1. Comparison between indoor RTLS technologies

Wireless technology	ZigBee	Wi-Fi	RFID		UWB
Frequency	868/915MHz 2.4GHz	2.4GHz	125KHz– 915MHz	2.4GHz	3.1GHz– 10.6GHz
Indoors accuracy	***	**	*	*	****
Detection range	***	**	*	**	*
Tag cost	**	**	***	**	*
Total cost	***	**	**	**	*
Ease of deployment	****	**	*	*	*
Tags autonomy	***	*	****	**	**
Tags size	**	**	***	**	**
Security	**	***	*	*	**

In Table 1, the main wireless technologies used for building indoor RTLSs have been compared according to different parameters, such as the indoors accuracy, the detection range, the costs and ease of deployment, the autonomy and size of the tags, as well as the security. In this table, one asterisk means the worst value, whilst four asterisks means the best value. For *tag cost* and *total cost*, a lower cost implies a higher rating. For *tags size*, a smaller size implies a higher rating. As can be seen, ZigBee provides a balanced set of features for implementing indoor RTLS, with a good accuracy, good tags autonomy, ease of deployment and reduced total cost [6]. Wi-Fi has the advantage of being an extended technology, but Wi-Fi tags have important problems of power consumption [4]. RFID tags are usually very cheap and small, and their power consumption is very low or even zero, but RFID readers have a reduced detection range and accuracy is very poor [3]. Finally, UWB provides the best indoors accuracy, but the total cost of these deployments is very expensive [5].

3   The n-Core Polaris Real-Time Locating System

Based on a set of target features that an RTLS should addresses, Nebusens and the BISITE Research Group have developed n-Core Polaris [7]. n-Core Polaris is an innovative indoor and outdoor Real-Time Locating System based on the n-Core platform [8] that features an outstanding precision, flexibility and automation integration [13]. n-Core Polaris exploits the potential of the n-Core platform, taking advantage of the advanced set of features of the n-Core Sirius devices and the n-Core Application Programming Interface [8].

The wireless infrastructure of n-Core Polaris is made up of several ZigBee nodes (i.e., tags, readers and sensor controllers) called n-Core Sirius A, Sirius B and Sirius D [8]. They all have 2.4GHz and 868/915MHz versions and include a USB port to charge their battery or supply them with power. Likewise, the USB port can be used to update the firmware of the devices and configure their parameters from a computer running a special application intended for it. On the one hand, n-Core Sirius B devices are intended to be used with an internal battery and include two general-purpose buttons. On the other hand, n-Core Sirius D devices are aimed at being used as fixed ZigBee routers using the main power supply through a USB adaptor. In the n-Core Polaris RTLS, n-Core Sirius B devices are used as tags, while n-Core Sirius D devices are used as readers. This way, n-Core Sirius B devices are carried by users and objects to be located, whereas n-Core Sirius D devices are placed at ceilings and walls to detect the tags. Finally, Sirius A devices incorporate several communication ports (GPIO, ADC, I2C and UART through USB or DB-9 RS-232) to connect to distinct devices, including almost every kind of sensor and actuator. All Sirius devices include an 8-bit RISC (Atmel ATmega 1281) microcontroller with 8KB of RAM, 4KB of EEPROM and 128KB of Flash memory and an IEEE 802.15.4/ZigBee transceiver (Atmel AT86RF230). Figure 1 shows a complete n-Core Development Kit including all these kinds of devices.

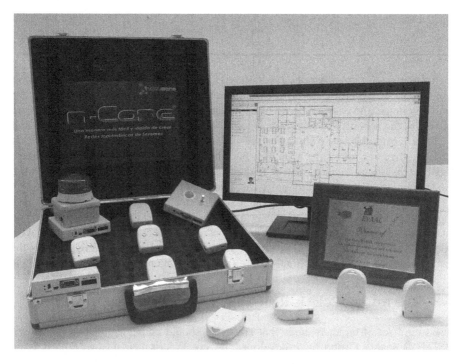

Fig. 1. n-Core Development Kit including n-Core Sirius B, Sirius D and Sirius A devices used as tags, readers and sensor controllers, respectively, in the n-Core Polaris Real-Time Locating System

In Figure 2 it can be seen the basic architecture of the n-Core Polaris Real-Time Locating System. The kernel of the system is a computer that is connected to a ZigBee network formed by n-Core Sirius devices. That is, the computer is connected to an n-Core Sirius D device through its USB port. This device acts as coordinator of the ZigBee network. The computer runs a web server module that makes use of a set of dynamic libraries, known as n-Core API (Application Programming Interface). The API offers the functionalities of the ZigBee network. The web server module offers a set of innovative locating techniques provided by the n-Core API. On the one hand, the computer gathers the detection information sent by the n-Core Sirius D acting as readers to the coordinator node. One the other hand, the computer acts as a web server offering the location info to a wide range of possible client interfaces. In addition, the web server module can access to a remote database to obtain information about the users and register historical data, such as alerts and location tracking.

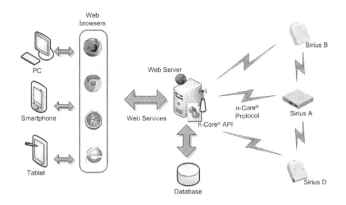

Fig. 2. Basic architecture of the n-Core Polaris RTLS

The operation of the system is as follows. Each user or object to be located in the system carries an n-Core Sirius B acting as tag. Each of these tags broadcasts periodically a data frame including, amongst other information, its unique identifier in the system. The rest of the time these devices are in a sleep mode, so that the power consumption is reduced. This way, battery lifetime can reach even several months, regarding the parameters of the system (broadcast period and transmission power). A set of n-Core Sirius D devices is used as readers throughout the environment, being placed on the ceiling and the walls. The broadcast frames sent by each tag are received by the readers that are close to them. This way, readers store in their memory a table with an entry per each detected tag. Each entry contains the identifier of the tag, as well as the RSSI (Received Signal Strength Indication) and the LQI (Link Quality Indicator) gathered from the broadcast frame reception. Periodically, each reader sends this table to the coordinator node connected to the computer. The coordinator forwards each table received from each reader to the computer through the USB port. Therefore, using all these detection information tables, the n-Core API, whose components are showed in Figure 3, applies a set of locating techniques to estimate the position of each tag in the monitored environment. These locating techniques include signpost, trilateration, as well as an innovative locating technique based on fuzzy logic [14].

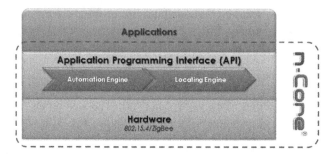

Fig. 3. Main components of n-Core, an integral hardware and software platform that includes ZigBee-based devices and an easy-to-use API including automation and location engines

Then, the web server module offers the location data to remote client interfaces as web services HTTP (Hypertext Transfer Protocol) over SOAP (Simple Object Access Protocol). This way, the n-Core Polaris system includes three basic client interfaces: a desktop application, a web application and a mobile application. Figure 4 shows a screenshot of the web client interface. This client interface has been designed to be simple, intuitive and easy-to-use. Administrator users can watch the position of all users and objects in the system in real-time through different interfaces. Furthermore, administrators can define restricted areas according to the users' permissions. This way, if some user enters in an area that is forbidden to it regarding its permissions, the system will generate an alert that is shown to the administrator through the client interfaces. In addition, such alerts are registered into the database, so administrators can check anytime if any user violated its permissions. Likewise, administrators can query the database to obtain the location track of a certain user, obtaining statistical measurements about its mobility or the most frequent areas where it moves.

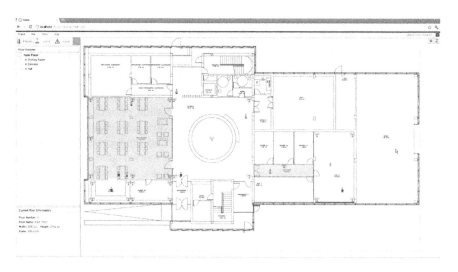

Fig. 4. Web client interface of the n-Core Polaris system

Furthermore, users can use one of the general-purpose buttons provided by the n-Core Sirius B devices to send an alert to the system. Similarly, administrators can send alerts from the system to a user of a set of users, which can confirm the reception using other of the buttons. The system not only provides locating features, but also scheduling and automation functionalities. The system can be easily integrated with a wide range of sensors and actuators using the variety of communication ports included in the n-Core Sirius A devices. By means of the automation engine provided by the n-Core API, the n-Core Polaris system can schedule automation tasks, as well as monitor all sensors in the environment in real-time. All the information can be accessed through the web client interfaces.

Even though the basic architecture of the n-Core Polaris RTLS describes how the n-Core API and the n-Core Sirius acting as coordinator are connected through a USB port, the modular and flexible architecture of the n-Core platform allows connecting the n-Core API to a set of n-Core Sirius devices using several virtual serial communication ports. This way, it is possible to connect a set of n-Core Sirius devices acting as data collecting nodes that are placed in distinct n-Core networks. The data connection is tunneled using, for example, RS-232 to Wi-Fi/Ethernet/3G converters (in fact, any kind of data transmission network is allowed), or directly using TCP/IP sockets. Therefore, n-Core Polaris can be used for locating users and assets in large n-Core networks or even n-Core networks remotely sited (e.g., a large hospital or even a set of different buildings belonging to the same healthcare entity), with users roaming from one n-Core network to another. Figure 5 depicts this architecture for large n-Core networks.

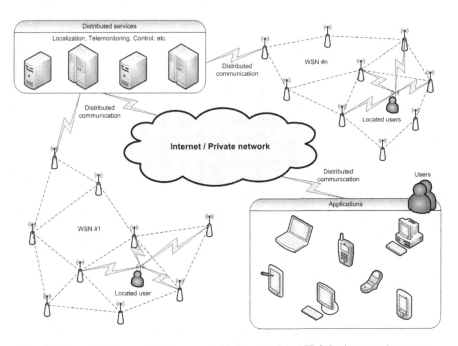

Fig. 5. The architecture and deployment of n-Core Polaris RTLS for large environments

To sum up, the main features and benefits of n-Core Polaris are:

- High scalability, thanks to the implementation of the IEEE 802.15.4/ZigBee international standard.
- Fast and simple deployment over the n-Core platform.
- Robust infrastructure that includes encryption and self-healing mechanisms against possible failures.
- Higher accuracy than other ZigBee-based Real-Time Locating Systems.
- Integration with sensors and actuators in the same infrastructure, which makes it a much more versatile alternative than other similar systems.
- Intuitive user interfaces that allow viewing the position of mobile elements in real-time, detecting accesses to restricted areas and managing alerts.
- Lower total cost compared with systems based on Wi-Fi or RFID, and much lower than those based on UWB.
- Higher tolerance to the presence of walls and obstacles than systems based on Wi-Fi and UWB.
- Sirius B devices provide much longer battery life (even months) compared with devices based on Wi-Fi and UWB.
- Its performance is not considerably affected by Wi-Fi networks, thanks to the network density and the greater number of used channels.
- Frequency band approved for its use in industrial and medical environments.
- Web Services based architecture that facilitates the integration of n-Core Polaris with a wide range of applications, including mobile interfaces.
- Capability to create your own RTLS by means of the n-Core API (Application Programming Interface).

4   Experiments and Results

The n-Core Polaris indoor locating system has been awarded as the winner of the first international competition on indoor localization and tracking [9], organized by the Ambient-Assisted Living Open Association (AALOA) [10] and performed in the Experimental Research Center in Applications and Services for Ambient Intelligence (CIAMI) [11], sited in the Technological Park of Valencia (Spain) and shown in Figure 6, from 27th to 29th July 2011. Among the competitors there were companies and research groups coming from all Europe, including Germany, Austria, France, Switzerland, Ukraine and Spain. Finally, the results were presented in Lecce (Italy) within the framework of the AAL Forum from 26th to 28th September 2011, with the participation of experts on Ambient-Assisted Living coming from all over the world.

In order to evaluate the competing localization systems, the following evaluation criteria were applied [9]. Each criterion had a maximum of 10 points. To calculate the overall score, each criterion was multiplied by a certain weight. As can be seen, the sum of the weights is *0.9*, thus the maximum overall score for a localization system would be *9*:

- *Accuracy (weight 0.25)*: each produced location sample was compared with the reference position, calculating the distance error. The final score on accuracy was the average between the scores obtained in the next two phases:

o   *Phase 1*: After a random walk the user stopped 30s in each Area of Interest (AoI). Accuracy was measured as the fraction of time in which the locating system provides the correct information.

o   *Phase 2*: The stream produced by competing systems was compared against a *logfile* of the expected position of the user. Specifically, the individual error of each measure was evaluated, and the 75th percentile of the errors was estimated.

Installation Complexity (0.2): a measure of the effort required to install the AAL locating system in a 70m^2 flat, measured by the evaluation committee as the total number of man-minutes of work needed to complete the installation. In this sense, the n-Core Polaris system was deployed in less than seven minutes in the flat, which demonstrates the ease of its installation.

User Acceptance (0.2): expresses how much the locating system is invasive in the user's daily life and thereby the impact perceived by the user; this parameter is qualitative and was evaluated by the evaluation committee.

Availability (0.15): fraction of time the locating system was active and responsive. It was measured as the ratio between the number of produced location data and the number of expected data (one sample every half a second).

Integrability into AAL Systems (0.1): use of open source solutions, use of standards, availability of developing libraries, integration with standard protocols.

In Figure 7 can be seen images of the deployment of the n-Core Sirius D devices used as readers throughout the CIAMI laboratory, as well as the n-Core Sirius B device used as tag during the competition (worn by the test user in his ankle).

Fig. 6. The Experimental Research Center in Applications and Services for Ambient Intelligence (CIAMI)

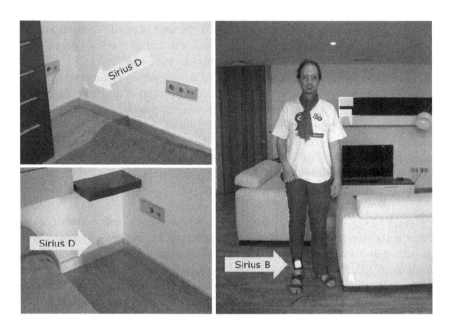

Fig. 7. Images of the deployment of the n-Core Sirius D devices used as readers and the n-Core Sirius B device used as tag during the EvAAL competition

For the competition, 15 readers were deployed throughout the CIAMI laboratory in less than 8 minutes, as can be seen in Figure 8.

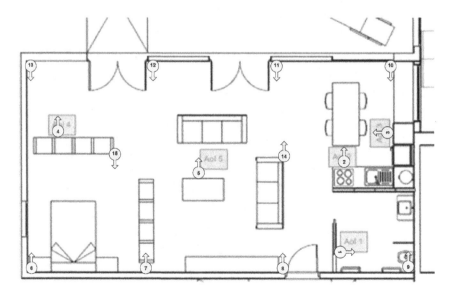

Fig. 8. Deployment of the n-Core Sirius D devices used as readers throughout the CIAMI laboratory

Figures 9, 10 and 11 show the performance of n-Core Polaris in the phase 2 when measuring accuracy. As can be seen, the n-Core Polaris system achieved a 0.97m mean distance error in the competition.

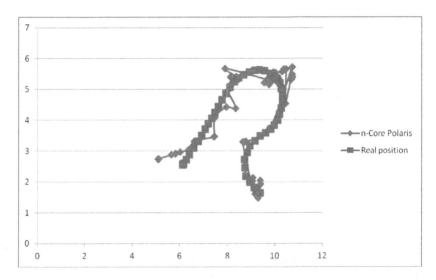

Fig. 9. Accuracy evaluation, phase 2, route 1 (Mean error = 0.777m; 3rd quartile = 1.056m)

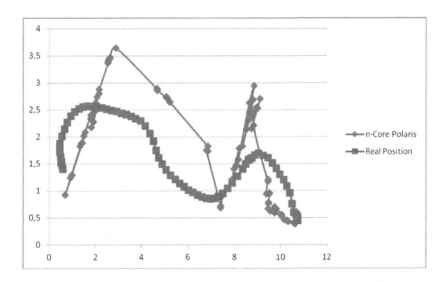

Fig. 10. Accuracy evaluation, phase 2, route 2 (Mean error = 1.055m; 3rd quartile = 1.306m)

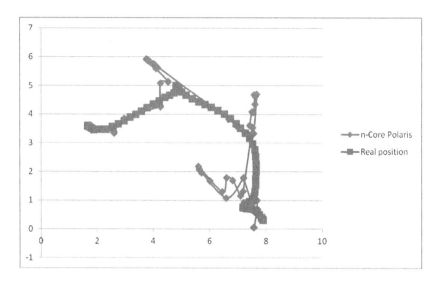

Fig. 11. Accuracy evaluation, phase 2, route 3 (Mean error = 1.088m; 3rd quartile = 1.338m)

As can be seen in Table 2, the n-Core Polaris system obtained the first place in the competition. These results demonstrate n-Core Polaris is a robust system suitable to be used in indoor environments, such as homes, hospitals or offices, and that can locate users and assets with up to 1m accuracy without interfering in the daily-life of people.

Table 2. Intermediate and overall scores of competitors in EvAAL Competition

Competitor	Accuracy	Availability	Installation Complexity	User Acceptance	Integrability in AAL	Overall Score
n-Core Polaris	5.9611	9.8756	10	7.625	6.5	7.14
AIT team	8.4540	1.3674	6.82	6.875	8.5	5.90
iLoc	7.8007	9.3922	0	5.875	4.5	4.98
OWLPS	1.3653	9.4337	8.4733	6.5	1	4.85
GEDES-UGR	1.8055	9.0193	0	6	10	4.00
SNTUmicro	0	0	10	4.375	3	3.17

5   Conclusions

Context-aware technologies, such as Wireless Sensor Networks, allow Ambient Assisted Living developments to automatically obtain information from users and their environment in a distributed and ubiquitous way. Among the wide range of Wireless Sensor Networks applications, Real-Time Locating Systems are emerging as one of the most exciting research areas. Healthcare, surveillance or work safety applications are only some examples of the possible environments where RTLSs can be exploited. There also are different wireless technologies that can be used on these systems. The ZigBee standard offers interesting features over the rest technologies, as it allows the use of large mesh networks of low-power devices and the integration with many other applications as it is an international standard using unlicensed frequency bands.

In this regard, the first International Competition on Indoor Localization and Tracking (EvAAL 2011) [9] is a very ambitious initiative in order to share knowledge among research groups and companies working on developing real AAAL-based systems and applications. From Nebusens and the BISITE Research Group of the University of Salamanca we are very proud to have participated in this event and will collaborate in future editions.

As demonstrated from the results of the EvAAL competition, n-Core Polaris provides an important competitive advantage to applications where it is necessary to know the location of people, animals or objects. Amongst its multiple application areas are the healthcare, the industrial or the agricultural sectors or even for emergency rescue operations [13], as well as those related to security and Ambient Assisted Living. Its optimal indoor and outdoor functioning makes n-Core Polaris a flexible, powerful and versatile solution.

Acknowledgments. This project has been supported by the Spanish Ministry of Science and Innovation (Subprograma Torres Quevedo).

References

1. Ambient Assisted Living Joint Programme, http://www.aal-europe.eu (accessed October 2011)
2. Nerguizian, C., Despins, C., Affès, S.: Indoor Geolocation with Received Signal Strength Fingerprinting Technique and Neural Networks. In: de Souza, J.N., Dini, P., Lorenz, P. (eds.) ICT 2004. LNCS, vol. 3124, pp. 866–875. Springer, Heidelberg (2004)
3. Tapia, D.I., de Paz, J.F., Rodríguez, S., Bajo, J., Corchado, J.M.: Multi-Agent System for Security Control on Industrial Environments. International Transactions on System Science and Applications Journal 4(3), 222–226 (2008)
4. Ding, B., Chen, L., Chen, D., Yuan, H.: Application of RTLS in Warehouse Management Based on RFID and Wi-Fi. In: 4th International Conference on Wireless Communications, Networking and Mobile Computing, WiCOM 2008, pp. 1–5 (2008)
5. Stelios, M.A., Nick, A.D., Effie, M.T., et al.: An indoor localization platform for ambient assisted living using UWB. In: Proceedings of the 6th International Conference on Advances in Mobile Computing and Multimedia, pp. 178–182. ACM, Linz (2008)
6. Liu, H., Darabi, H., Banerjee, P., Liu, J.: Survey of Wireless Indoor Positioning Techniques and Systems. IEEE Trans. Syst. Man Cybern. Part C-Appl. Rev. 37, 1067–1080 (2007)
7. Nebusens, n-Core® Polaris: An innovative Real-Time Locating System that Features an Outstanding Precision, Flexibility and Automation Integration (2012), http://www.n-core.info/polaris (accessed April 2012)
8. Nebusens, n-Core®: A Faster and Easier Way to Create Wireless Sensor Networks (2011), http://www.n-core.info (accessed April 2012)

9. AAL Open Association, Evaluating AAL Systems through Competitive Benchmarking (2011), `http://evaal.aaloa.org` (accessed October 2011)
10. AALOA, AAL Open Association (2010), `http://www.aaloa.org` (accessed April 2012)
11. CIAMI Living Lab., Experimental Research Center in Applications and Services for Ambient Intelligence (2009), `http://www.ciami.es` (accessed April 2012)
12. Kaemarungsi, K., Krishnamurthy, P.: Modeling of indoor positioning systems based on location fingerprinting. In: INFOCOM 2004. Twenty-third Annual Joint Conference of the IEEE Computer and Communications Societies, vol. 2, pp. 1012–1022 (2004)
13. García, Ó., Alonso, R.S., Tapia, D.I., Guevara, F., de la Prieta, F., Bravo, R.A.: A Maritime Piracy Scenario for the n-Core Polaris Real-Time Locating System. In: Omatu, S., Paz Santana, J.F., González, S.R., Molina, J.M., Bernardos, A.M., Rodríguez, J.M.C. (eds.) Distributed Computing and Artificial Intelligence. AISC, vol. 151, pp. 601–608. Springer, Heidelberg (2012)
14. De Paz, J.F., Tapia, D.I., Alonso, R.S., Pinzón, C.I., Bajo, J., Corchado, J.M.: Mitigation of the Ground Reflection Effect in Real-Time Locating Systems Based on Wireless Sensor Networks by Using Artificial Neural Networks. In: Knowledge and Information Systems. Springer, London (2012), doi:10.1007/s10115-012-0479-8

Author Index

Alonso, Ricardo S.   92
Arredondo, Maria Teresa   14

Barsocchi, Paolo   1, 14
Braun, Andreas   26
Bravo, Raúl A.   92

Canalda, Philippe   36
Catalina, Jorge   92
Corchado, Juan M.   92
Cypriani, Matteo   36

Furfari, Francesco   1

García, Óscar   92
Garrido, José Luis   65
Gil, Alejandro M. Medrano   1
Guevara, Fabio   92

Heggen, Henning   26

Jost, Christian   52

Kaufmann, Lukas   52
Kistler, Rolf   52
Klapproth, Alexander   52
Knauth, Stefan   52

Noguera, Manuel   65

Potortì, Francesco   1

Ramos, Juan Pablo Làzaro   14
Rodríguez-Domínguez, Carlos   65
Ruiz-López, Tomás   65

Salvi, Dario   14
Shirokov, Igor   80
Spies, François   36

Tapia, Dante I.   92

Wichert, Reiner   26